STREET COP

To Tom, a good street cop.

STREET
COP

Innovative Tactics
for Taking Back
the Streets

Donovan Jacobs

Paladin Press
Boulder, Colorado

Street Cop:
Innovative Tactics for Taking Back the Streets
by Donovan Jacobs

Cover illustration by Bill Border.

CONTENTS

ACKNOWLEDGMENTS

y strength and field specialty has always been narcotics, and you'll note that bias throughout this book. Narcotics enforcement provides the greatest contact with street criminals because drugs are the number one cause of crime. There are areas of street work, however, that I was weak in. To compensate for this weakness, I contacted officers known to be strong in these particular areas for their input. This input, I believe, makes *Street Cop* a thorough composition on street police work.

I would like to thank San Diego Police Department (SDPD) Officer James E. Stevens for his overall review of the book and, in particular, his help on the chapters on auto theft and gangs. Los Angeles Police Department (LAPD) Officer Bill Parker provided enormous assistance in the editing process, as well as a well-seasoned critique of its contents. SDPD Sergeant Tony Johnson's constructive criticism on overall content and format was greatly appreciated. SDPD Sergeant Dennis Johnson's humorous editing and pointed critiques were helpful in bringing a training officer's perspective to the book. SDPD Detective Jack Haeussinger's input made sure the book was up to date and kept me honest on legal fine points. SDPD Detective Ron Featherly provided helpful hints on suspect interrogation. SDPD Detective Mike Gallivan's response ensured the accuracy of the text and affirmed the need for such a book.

Thanks, guys.

■ PREFACE

 **treet Cop** \stret kop\ n., 1. A police officer knowledgeable in the habits and criminal behavior patterns of the street criminal, including convicts, junkies, and gang members. 2. adj., A title of respect given to a police officer by his peers.

This book is about the techniques and tactics a patrol officer needs to employ in order to actively identify, locate, and arrest criminal suspects. It begins with a review of the critical legal basics necessary to sustain a proper arrest. The procedures used to identify criminals are discussed next, followed by tactics to apprehend fleeing suspects. The text ends with information on how to recognize hard-core street criminals, conduct patrol criminal investigations, and handle proactive arrest techniques.

The police academy teaches you to operate a microphone, write a report, put bullets in paper targets, and fingerprint window panes. Your series of training officers refine what you have learned in the academy and teach you how to apply that knowledge on patrol. This instruction teaches you which laws are enforced and which are not, what type of work product is expected, and the nuts and bolts of radio call responses. Little time is spent teaching criminal behavior recognition or arrest tactics.

A rookie officer enters the field insecure in his criminal apprehension abilities. His focus is on radio calls and traffic citations to generate activity. He feels secure in these areas because neither requires much imagination or confidence to handle. Few officers are ever adequately trained in the proactive street tactics necessary to actually solve a crime, arrest a criminal, or address a problem area.

Years on the streets will eventually provide the the necessary on-the-job training to accomplish the goal of effective criminal apprehension. However, most officers either leave the job or are promoted off the street prior to gaining this street knowledge.

This book is intended to condense years of street experience into a format that will educate a young officer in aggressive criminal apprehension techniques. *All* of the stories used to illustrate the lessons in this book are true. And these proven techniques work on the "streets."

Although this book contains the experience of a number of excellent street cops who put in years of street police work, it does not profess to cover it all. If you feel this book is missing a trick or tactic you have successfully employed, I would like to know about it.

Send the information to me in care of Paladin Press, P.O. Box 1307, Boulder, CO, 80306, and I'll review it for publication in future editions. You'll receive an acknowledgment in the new edition. The key to this book is credibility among street cops. This can best be supported by continual revision and active input from street cops.

There is no reason an officer needs to rely on radio

calls or traffic citations for activity generation. *Street Cop* provides the necessary information to enable an officer to leave the station with the confidence and knowledge to lock crooks up aggressively. Good luck, good hunting, and be careful out there.

CHAPTER 1

LEARN TO PLAY THE LEGAL GAME BY THE RULES

Graveyard, 0300; the change-of-shift rush is over and the two-hour-old disturbance calls are cleared. All the drunks are home safe in bed, and the streets are empty. It's time to play park ranger.

Your beat is 25 square miles of Southern California middle class residential housing. The community has built up progressively to the point where the only remaining open space consists of carefully manicured city parks. They are eight in number, and they are your only consistent source of activity after 2 A.M. Each one is on your graveyard tour. Some nights' activity is better than others, but for the most part, one circuit of the parks usually generates an arrest or two.

You drive purposefully from one park to another looking for drug use, vandals, and passed-out teenagers. The parking lots are your main targets in this nightly hunt, but then it extends to the open areas. You gain access to these areas via the narrow concrete sidewalks obviously placed there for your use.

Your sidewalk driving skills have improved considerably over the course of this three-month graveyard shift. It's gotten to the point now where on any one night your sprinkler head damage count is only one per lap. Go-kart racing comes to mind as you traverse the course.

You enter the parking lot of a park named after a dead president and drive toward the sole physical structure—the rest room/storage building. The building sits at the end of a hundred-yard-long strip of sidewalk. You catch a glimpse of a figure moving quickly to the opposite side of the structure.

This is where all the midnight sidewalk driving practice comes into play. The grass is always wet, and straying onto the grass as you accelerate will destroy the ground cover and send you slipping down the gentle slope. Expertly, you maneuver your black and white over the twisting ribbon of concrete toward the building.

Now comes the almost unthinkable. You will have to park and actually leave your vehicle and walk a distance greater than 20 feet. You hope that the amount of caffeine and sugar you have stocked up on at the 24-hour health-food store (Winchell's Donuts) will help you survive this endurance test. Rounding the corner of the building on foot, you find yourself outnumbered six to one by a group of teenage thrill seekers.

You place a call for assistance over your walkie-talkie. From the sleepy response of responding unit 611 Y, Officer Parker, you calculate that you have about eight minutes of tap dancing ahead of you while you attempt to maintain control of these delinquents.

You quickly evaluate your legal standing. The individuals in the group all appear to be under 18. Your city has imposed a ten o'clock curfew for juveniles, so the detention and possible arrest of these violators is permissible. You direct all six to line up against the building, and you begin discussing their activities of the evening. The second

subject from the end quickly distin-
guishes himself from the others by
developing an "attitude." It seems Mr.
Attitude is offended that a police offi-

cer would dare question his activities at 0300 in a dark-
ened residential park. Mr. Attitude's negative vibes appear
to be catching on, and you realize this brushfire of opposi-
tion needs to be quelled immediately.

You make note of their bulky, dark jackets and the
potential for concealed weapons. With a legitimate concern for your safety, you order all hands on the wall. This
show of authority quiets the youngsters.

Your cover unit arrives, and you begin to pat down the
subjects in a search for weapons. Mr. Attitude is first. You
feel a hard, unusually shaped object in the right coat pocket. Believing legitimately that it could be a weapon, you
remove it. It seems Mr. Attitude has been raiding his mother's kitchen drawers, and you have in your hand a fork.

This is not, however, an ordinary fork. Mr. Attitude
has been watching Uri Geller, the famous utensil-ben-
der/magician, and he has manipulated the fork into a
hideous-looking weapon. The tines are bent away from
the handle like the spread of a peacock's feathers. The
handle, covered by gauze and tape, is folded back against
itself, forming a hand-hold. The device is designed to be
held like brass knuckles, with the tines used to strike the
intended victim. As impressed as you are with Mr. Attitude's ingenuity, you place him under arrest for possession of brass knuckles, a felony.

You feel good about the arrest. While most officers are
tending to late-night car shopping at the local car dealer
or catching up on world events at the emergency room,
you have been scouring your beat for criminals. Your
effort has resulted in a quality arrest accomplished
through aggressive proactive tactics. You feel you have
followed all legal guidelines properly, and you start on
the arrest report.

Your arrest report reflects the chronology of the
night's events and culminates with a description of
your concerns for your personal safety (the late hour,
the ratio of six individuals to two officers, the hostility

of the subjects, the bulky jackets).

After the arrest, your investigation reveals that the suspect is 18, an adult. He cannot be charged with curfew violation, but you feel you have the legal basis for the pat-down well covered. The district attorney (DA) also thinks so and issues the case.

The one person whose opinion on this issue really counts, however, disagrees. The judge has an exacting knowledge of search-and-seizure law and recognizes a fatal flaw in your rationale for the pat-down. The law on such matters specifies that there must be objective reason(s) to believe the subject of the pat-down has a weapon. A generalized suspicion or a generalized fear for one's safety is not due cause. Specific facts supporting such a belief might be an admission to having a weapon, the outline of a knife in a pocket, witness statements, and so on.

The judge declares the pat-down improper and, therefore, the subsequent discovery of the brass knuckles as well. The brass knuckles are not allowed in evidence, and the charges are dropped.

* * * * *

The key to street work is knowing what you can do and when you can do it. What you learned in the academy is only a skeleton of the actual law. Street work requires a fine-tuned knowledge of criminal law and criminal procedure. This knowledge is especially critical to aggressive, proactive-type police work.

The following information is directly related to street work. It focuses on the areas of law that patrol officers have the most difficulty in assimilating and using in real life. This information is not intended to provide an all-encompassing view of criminal law, but to expand and reinforce what patrol officers should know and understand.

THE STOP

Patrol officers have been told time and again that a "stop and frisk" has to be justified by a "reasonable suspicion" that a crime is occurring and that this individual may be responsible for it. So why do many continue to write, "I observed Smith standing at

the corner of 38th and Hemlock at 2 A.M. This corner is a high-crime area known for drug sales. I contacted Smith. He was wearing a bulky jacket, and, fearing for my safety, I patted him down for weapons. I felt a bulge in his coat pocket. I removed the item, and it was a baggie of "rock" cocaine. I arrested Smith." This is a prime example of an illegal detention, illegal search, and thus, an arrest unsupported by legally admissible evidence.

In the academy you are taught to observe and articulate your reasons for stopping someone. These reasons are supposed to establish a reasonable suspicion that this person is involved in criminal conduct. A stop occurs when the individual is not free to leave. A subject being questioned by the police or field interviewed is not free to leave. You know it, the defense attorney knows it, and the judge knows it. If an officer hasn't satisfied the legal requirement of establishing a reasonable suspicion for the stop and an arrest results, the district attorney will either throw the case out or the defense will make a valid motion to have it dismissed.

We all know the rules, so why don't we abide by them? Sometimes circumstances won't allow it. Events are happening quickly, safety is paramount, and there are honest mistakes. No problem. However, after a few "hit and runs," a good cop knows what the pattern will be. The ones "holding" drop the dope, the ones "high" try to amble away, and the bold hang out.

Street Tip: The smart cop is ready for this pattern. He watches first and then contacts. He watches the hands and waits for the littering to occur. He looks to see if the subject with the beer appears underage and then stops him. The sophisticated cop watches for visible but often subtle objective symptoms of drug use, then he stops the subject. Each of these stops meet the legal requirements of a reasonable suspicion necessary to justify a stop or detention. Get used to looking for minor law violations to establish the reason-

able suspicion to justify the routine field interview which may turn into a good felony arrest.

THE PAT-DOWN

Now that a proper foundation has been laid for the detention, the search has to be justified. You need reasonable suspicion that this individual possesses a weapon to justify a pat-down of his exterior clothing. A pat-down is considered a limited search. It takes more than a nondescript bulge to establish a reasonable suspicion. An outline of a knife in a jeans pocket, the appearance of the tip of a leather sheath at the coat's edge, even a statement from the subject will suffice.

The reality of the streets is that almost anyone contacted by the police is patted down. Safety being paramount, it is common sense to do so, regardless of legal fine lines. However, taking time to plan and observe, even for a moment, will turn that illegal search into one that is legally acceptable.

Street Tip: At the beginning of the contact, ask the subject if he has any weapons on his person. A common response is "just a pocket knife." This is the reasonable suspicion you need to remove the knife during the pat-down. Keep in mind you will want to continue the pat-down after the recovery of the "pocket knife" for additional weapons. The continuance of the pat-down must be supported by your training and experience that tell you people with weapons often possess more than one. This knowledge provides the reasonable suspicion necessary to continue the pat-down.

WARNING: Sometimes when the suspect is asked if he has a weapon, his natural reaction is to reach for it. Be prepared to stop a reaching suspect.

BULGES

A common discovery on a pat-down search is the

nondescript bulge. Since this bulge cannot be discerned as a possible weapon, as an officer in a nonarrest situation, you cannot remove and

examine the object legally. However, you can ask the subject what the bulge is. His response may provide the probable cause necessary for an arrest, which allows you to remove the object.

Suppose you have stopped a young man for not having a bicycle license and notice a buck knife in a sheath on his belt. You remove the knife and conduct a pat-down for additional weapons. You feel a bulge in his jacket pocket. You ask, "What is this?"

He states it's "only weed." You know from training and experience that "weed" is slang for marijuana. You then place him under arrest for possession of marijuana, then reach into the coat and seize the item. It turns out to be a film canister of marijuana. This was a proper stop, pat-down, arrest, and search, and this is the way your arrest report should read.

Keep in mind it was *not* necessary to advise him of his constitutional rights prior to your question. Although he is not free to leave, he is detained due to the traffic code violation. You are not asking him a question regarding specific criminal conduct. Thus, you do not need to advise him of his constitutional rights.

Another avenue you may take in order to seize the bulge is formulating a proper opinion as to what the item is and then making an arrest based on that opinion. An arrest must be based on probable cause. Probable cause is that evidence which would lead an officer with similar training and experience to conclude the object is contraband. Evidence is anything open to the senses, including sight, smell, hearing, and touch. If any of these provide probable cause, the item may then be removed and seized legally.

For example, a proper pat-down reveals a bulge in a subject's front pants pocket. You know from numerous arrests that this bulge feels like a hypodermic syringe. You can tell by the shape, hardness, and size of the object that it is a syringe. You place the subject under arrest for possession of a syringe then remove it. Critical in this type of an arrest is your prior experience with syringes. Be sure to outline the number of times you have encountered these items in your arrest report.

Street Tip: Police cars equipped with cages usually have removable backseats that allow an officer to check for abandoned contraband. An officer suspecting a bullet may be contraband may wish to make available to a suspect or detainee this controlled disposal site. Place the subject in the backseat, let it be known he will soon be searched thoroughly, and then give him some privacy. Upon removal of the suspect, search the backseat area.

In order to ensure that any contraband found under the seat belongs to the suspect, be sure to have searched it after the last detainee. Your report must also state the car has been in your exclusive control during the entire period following your last backseat search. Finally, describe the bulge you felt in the suspect's clothing initially and the fact it is no longer there.

VEHICLE SEARCHES

Under the "movable vehicle" exception to the search warrant requirement, an officer may usually search a vehicle without a warrant if there is probable cause to believe it contains contraband or evidence. Probable cause is that amount of evidence which would lead a reasonable person to believe the vehicle contains such contraband.

An exception is when you have a suspect in a vehicle and you have at least a reasonable suspicion that he has a weapon. Then it is permissible to conduct a search of the vehicle within "arm's reach" of the suspect to ensure he does not arm himself.

Street Tip: Evidence needed to search a car may be the odor of burning marijuana, the odor of PCP, the odor of an alcoholic beverage, the plastic orange cap for a syringe, a marijuana "roach," a cartridge, or an empty holster. The evidence you need to search is anything that would lead you to believe the car contains additional contraband (e.g., a gun, drugs, an illegal syringe).

CONSENT SEARCHES

An underutilized legal ground for searches is the consent search. Simply asking a suspect for permission to search his person, car, or home is legally acceptable. However, there are a couple of warnings that go along with such searches.

First, asking every motorist for permission to search

Pay close attention to areas of vehicles often containing contraband. Ashtrays commonly contain marijuana roaches, and gloveboxes are used to stash weapons or other drugs. In this case, the marijuana roach shown gives probable cause to search the entire vehicle for additional marijuana.

his vehicle on a traffic stop is not going to be allowed. Judges are leery of consent searches because subtle coercion may be used in obtaining them. To alleviate such concerns, be able to articulate why you were seeking consent. What were your suspicions pointing to this individual that warranted asking permission for a search?

Be aware of the physical and mental circumstances under which the consent is obtained. Guns should be holstered or out of sight, the number of officers present

---

NARCOTIC TASK FORCE

CONSENT TO SEARCH PREMISES

Case No._____

Date_____

I, _____, having been informed of my constitutional right not to have a search made on the premises hereinafter mentioned without a search warrant, and of my right to refuse to consent to such a search, hereby authorizes _____ and _____ _____ Police Officer(s) of the City of _____ to conduct a complete search of my premises located at _____ _____ in the City of San Diego, California. These Officers are authorized by me to take from my premises any letters, papers, materials, contraband, or other property which they may desire.

This written permission is being given by me to the above named Police Officers voluntarily and without coercion, threats, or promises of any kind.

_____

_____

_____
Witnesses

Carry consent-to-search forms with your clipboard. Although such searches are often challenged, frequent use will educate an officer on the legal fine lines that will ensure that the search is upheld as proper.

should be limited if possible, the situation should be under control (no doors being kicked in, kids crying hysterically, multiple demands being made,

etc.), and a standard written consent form should be utilized. Ideally, the situation should be calm and relaxed. Be prepared to articulate such conditions in your report.

Street Tip: Carry written consent forms with you. Their use assists you in establishing that consent was given both knowingly and voluntarily. Both conditions

Reporting Department		Beat Number		Date / Time of Report		Notice of Stored Vehicle Delivered Personally ☐ To:		Case Number	

Location Towed / Stolen / Recovered from	Odometer Reading	VIN Clear in SVS? ☐ Yes ☐ No	Date / Time Dispatch Notified
		LIC Clear in SVS? ☐ Yes ☐ No	

License Number	One ☐ Two ☐	State	Plate Type	Exp. (Mo / Year)	Vehicle Identification Number	Engine Number

Year	Make	Model	Body Type	Color Combination /	Appraised Value ☐ 0-300 ☐ 301-1000 ☐ 1000+	Owner Valuation $

Condition	Yes	No	Items	Yes	No	Items	Yes	No	Tires / Wheels	Condition	Items	Identification Number
Wrecked			Seat (Front)			Driving Lights			Left Front		Camper	
Burned			Seat (Rear)			Registration			Right Front		Cargo	
Vandalized			Radio			Alt / Generator			Left Rear		Vessel as Load	
Eng / Trans Strip			Tape Deck			Battery			Right Rear		Firearms	
Misc. Parts Strip			Tapes (#)			Differential			Spare		Radio / Tape Deck	
Body Metal Strip			Other Stereo			Transmission			Hub Caps (#)		Stereo	
Doors Locked			Car Phone			Automatic			Special Wheels		Car Phone	
Ignition Locked			Ignition Key			Tampered Ignition					Other	

Vehicle Damage

TOP   LEFT SIDE   FRONT   REAR   RIGHT SIDE

Identifying Marks, Damage, Interior (Describe Color(s). If Customized, Etc.) Continue in Narrative As Necessary	Insurance Carrier

CURRENT / REGISTERED OWNER	LEGAL OWNER

Name (Last, First, Middle)	Name (Last, First, Middle)

Street Address	Apt. / Suite #	Street Address	Apt. / Suite #

City	State	Zip	City	State	Zip

Phone Day ( )	Night ( )	Phone Day ( )	Night ( )

☐ STORED ☐ IMPOUNDED ☐ RELEASED ☐ RECOVERED – VEHICLE / COMPONENT

Towing Storage Concern (Name, Address, Phone)	Towed To / Stored At:

Storage Authority and Reason	Drivable ☐ No ☐ Yes ☐ Unk	VIN Appears Altered / Removed ☐ Yes ☐ No / VIN Switched ☐ Yes ☐ No / VIN Matches Registration Card ☐ Yes ☐ No

Release Vehicle To: ☐ R / O Agent ☐ Agency Hold	Garage Principal or Agent Storing Vehicle (Signature) X	Date	Time

Name of Person Authorizing Release (Print)	Date	Certification: I, the Undersigned, Do Hereby Certify that I Am Legally Authorized and Entitled to Take Possession of the Above Described Vehicle.

Signature of Person Authorizing Release X	X Signature of Person Taking Possession

☐ STOLEN VEHICLE / COMPONENT ☐ EMBEZZLED VEHICLE ☐ PLATE(S) REPORT

Date and Time of Occurrence	Name of Reporting Party	Driver's License	State

Home Address	Telephone ( )	Business Address	Telephone ( )

Last Driver of Vehicle	Date	Time	Address	Telephone ( )

I Certify or Declare Under the Laws of the State of California That the Foregoing is True and Correct.	Signature of Person Making Stolen Report X	Date	Time

Reporting Officer	I.D. #	Division	Approved By	I.D. #	Detective(s) Assigned	I.D. #

Required Notices sent to Registered and Legal Owners Per 22852 CVC	☐ Yes ☐ No	Date Notified	Validation Notice Sent	☐ Yes ☐ No	Date Notified

The requirements of an inventory search allow access to the entire vehicle. Be sure to follow your department's policy on every impound to avoid accusations the search and impound was merely a pretext to search the vehicle.

are necessary for a valid consent search. The forms also provide a format by which you are placed in a position to request permission calmly and diplomatically. This structured delivery teaches you successful persuasion techniques effective in gaining consent. Finally, be sure you read the signature to prevent Mickey Mouse from authorizing the search.

IMPOUND SEARCHES

Some states have statutes allowing officers to impound a vehicle driven by an individual who has had his license suspended or never had a license. Career criminals often fall into this category. State statutes then allow for an inventory search of the vehicle before it is impounded.

A street cop should take full advantage of these laws. First, a junkie or gang member on foot is less criminally active. Second, the inventory search is perfectly legal cause to search a criminal's vehicle completely. Understand that impounding a car cannot be used as a pretext to search a car. You must follow department policies consistently with regard to this area to avoid this problem.

Street Tip: A suspect who is lying about his name is not going to have a driver's license on record. This is legal cause to then search and impound his vehicle. Once arrested for not having a license, the suspect can then be transported to the station to begin the identification process.

TELEPHONIC SEARCH WARRANTS

Often searches of residences are preceded by the discovery of contraband within the residence during a routine radio call, which makes your presence there lawful. In order to conduct an in-depth search of the house, however, you will need a search warrant or consent. Telephonic search warrants are the easiest for a patrol officer to obtain. This generally requires a phone call to an on-duty deputy district attorney, then a recorded

three-way call to an on-call judge.
After service of the warrant, the officer meets with the judge the next day
to file the search warrant and to

return the "inventory and receipt" form. In order to facilitate the process of obtaining a telephonic search warrant
and to reduce the "hassle" involved, carry the simple
forms with you.

Another reason to carry the forms is to assist you in
persuading the resident to consent to a search of his residence. Demonstrating that you are prepared to obtain a
warrant often will be enough to convince the resident
you are not bluffing.

Be careful when presenting your case. Simply state
you have probable cause to obtain a warrant and you will
do so if you do not obtain consent. Do not use language
that may be viewed as threatening. This will invalidate
any consent you may receive. Subterfuge—stating that
you have probable cause for the search when you don't—
is not allowed either.

The key to smoothing out the telephonic search warrant process is finding a location you're comfortable
with to make necessary phone calls. A phone booth is
going to be more trouble than it's worth. Use the phone
at the residence if at all possible; if not, use a neighbor's
or the station's.

Prepare a complete rough of the affidavit before calling the assistant district attorney. Anticipate the obvious
questions and be prepared to answer them. The first will
be whether you have asked for consent. Others will focus
on the initial reason for the contact, the "plain sight"
observation, and your expertise.

SEARCH-AND-SEIZURE WAIVERS

Search-and-seizure waivers, also known as Fourth
Amendment waivers, are frequently conditions of probation. These waivers allow the search of a defendant, his
car, and his home at any time by any police officer. The
only limitation on such searches are that they not be
done for harassment purposes.

Information on who has such a waiver is in the defendant's case file relating to the crime he was convicted of and with his probation officer. The original case file is maintained at the county courthouse where the case was adjudicated. It contains a copy of the original complaint, court orders, sentencing, and proba-

---

MUNICIPAL COURT OF CALIFORNIA

SAN DIEGO JUDICIAL DISTRICT

LONG FORM DRUG PROBATION CONDITIONS

You have been Sentenced by the Court but this Sentence has been suspended for a period of _____ years if you obey the following terms and conditions of your probation.

YOU ARE ORDERED TO:

1. Not possess any dangerous drugs or narcotics unless prescribed for you by a licensed physician;

2. Submit your person, property, vehicle and residence to search and seizure at any time of day or night by any enforcement officer with or without a warrant;

3. Submit to Nalline and/or Urinalysis tests whenever required by your Probation Officer or any Peace Officer;

4. Not cross the International Border into the Republic of Mexico;

5. Not associate with known users or traffickers in narcotics or dangerous drugs;

6. Not be convicted of a same or similar offense.

I acknowledge that I have read and understand these conditions of my Court ordered probation and that failure to obey them may result in the revocation of my probation.

DATED:_____   _____
                                     DEFENDANT'S SIGNATURE

A common condition for drug-related probation is the defendant's waiver of his Fourth Amendment rights. (The second condition listed on this form is very straightforward and is a very strong enforcement tool for police officers.)

tion conditions, and it is filed by number. The number is available under the defendant's name through the computerized criminal history file

or through a printed index available to the public at the court clerk's office. Misdemeanor cases are filed with the municipal court clerk and felony cases with the superior court clerk.

Some police departments have search-and-seizure waiver information available in printed indexes and in the computerized criminal history files. Keep in mind parolees are subject to different rules and a police officer does not have carte blanche to search them. You must go through their parole officer and he must direct you to do the search. You cannot ask the parole officer for permission to search. He must request your assistance on his own.

RAMEY

Under the Ramey decision, an arrest in a person's home without a warrant is illegal. There are, however, several notable exceptions:

Exigent Circumstances

Fresh pursuit of a suspect into his residence does not require any type of warrant. Under other exigent circumstances (e.g., evidence being destroyed, persons being injured), an arrest is permissible as long as the officer did not create the exigency.

Search-and-Seizure Waivers

A suspect subject to a search and seizure waiver conditions may be searched and arrested in his own residence without a warrant as long as probable cause exists for the arrest.

Arrest Warrants

Arresting a suspect on outstanding warrants is permissible within his own residence. Other charges then may be added when he is booked into jail. Be prepared to explain how the residence and the defendant were connected.

No Probable Cause Exists
If you intend to contact a subject for an interview regarding a crime and you do not have probable cause to arrest,

---

COUNTY OF KERN, STATE OF CALIFORNIA

ARREST WARRANT
["RAMEY WARRANT"]

THE PEOPLE OF THE STATE OF CALIFORNIA,
TO ANY PEACE OFFICER:

WARRANT NO.:_____
(Case number)

Proof by declaration under penalty of perjury having been made this day to me by

_____, I find that there is probable cause to believe
[Name of Officer]

[ ] MISD.
that the crime(s) of _____
[ ] FELONY
[List Crime(s)]

were committed on or about _____/_____/19_____
[List Date(s) of Offense(s)]

by the defendant named and described below.

THEREFORE, YOU ARE COMMANDED TO ARREST: _____
[Name of Defendant(s)]

and to bring said defendant before any magistrate in Kern County pursuant to Penal Code Sections 821, 825, 826 and 848. In lieu of bring said defendant before a magistrate, you may release said defendant from custody, prior to the time limitations of Penal Code Section 825, without bail and without further appearance before a magistrate.

Defendant is to be admitted to bail in the amount of $ _____

Time Issued:_____[a.m./p.m.]   _____
[Signature of the Judge]

Dated:_____/____/ 19____   Judge of the _____ Court

[MISDEMEANORS] GOOD CAUSE HAVING BEEN SHOWN by affidavit, this warrant may be served at anytime of the day or night, as approved by my initials:_____
****
DESCRIPTION OF DEFENDANT

Sex _____ Race _____ D.O.B. _____ Height _____ Weight _____

Hair _____ Eyes _____ Scars/Marks/Tattos _____

License/I.D.# _____ SSN _____ LAR # _____

Residence Address _____
[#/Street/City/State]

Vehicle: Year _____ Make _____ Model _____ Color _____
Info.& :
Desc. : License # _____ State _____

Other Information: _____

* [The complaint underlying this warrant of arrest does not initiate a criminal]
[proceeding. See People v. Ramey (1976) 16 Cal.3d 263 and People v. Sesslin]
[(1968) 68 Cal.2d 418, 425-427, fn. 6.   ]
KCDA 4/87

In some jurisdictions, easily obtained "Ramey Arrest Warrants" are available to officers prior to a case being issued by the district attorney's office. The process to obtain one is similar to that of a telephonic search warrant.

then consensual contact in the residence is permissible. If during this contact you establish probable cause to arrest, then an arrest in the residence is permissible.

COUNTY OF KERN, STATE OF CALIFORNIA

PROBABLE CAUSE COMPLAINT IN SUPPORT OF ARREST WARRANT *
[DECLARATION IN SUPPORT OF THE "RAMEY WARRANT"]

I, _____, declare under penalty of perjury:

I am employed as a _____ by the _____.
                        [Position]   [Department]

I have probable cause to arrest _____
                                  [Name of Suspect(s)]

for the following crime(s):_____
                                [List Crimes]

[CHECK THE APPROPRIATE BOXES AND PROVIDE ATTACHMENTS]

_____   Attached to this declaration and incorporated by reference is a written statement of facts which I have prepared. The facts set forth in this written statement are true, based upon my information and belief, except for those facts which are set forth as my own observations, which I know to be true based upon personal knowledge.

_____   Attached to this declaration and incorporated by reference are offense reports, which are official records of the _____. I have personally reviewed each of these written reports. The facts set forth in these offense reports are true, based upon my information and belief, except for those facts which are set forth as my own observations, which I know to be true based upon personal knowledge.

_____   Incorporated in this declaration by reference is my oral affidavit to the Honorable _____ at approximately _____ [a.m./p.m.] on _____/_____/19____. This oral affidavit [in support of a search warrant] was recorded. The original tape recording will be filed with the clerk of the _____ Court.

I declare under penalty of perjury that the foregoing is true and correct.
Executed at _____, California on _____/_____/19____

_____
[Signature of Officer]

_____
[Print or Type Name of Officer]

*[The complaint underlying this warrant of arrest does not initiate a criminal]
[proceeding. See People v. Ramey (1976) 16 Cal.3d 263 and People v. Sesslin]
[(1968) 86 Cal.2d 418, 425-427, fn. 6.   ]

Probable Cause Exists

If probable cause exists to arrest the subject but you do not intend to arrest in the residence, contact is permitted. For example, you have identified a suspect in a prescription forgery case and you need a handwriting exemplar for comparison purposes. The suspect is elderly and booking into jail is not necessary. You may contact the suspect at his residence, ask for the exemplar, and then leave without making an arrest. To prevent confusion, you should tell them they are not under arrest, and you will not arrest them.

Subterfuge

Subterfuge is permitted to lure a suspect, whom you have probable cause to arrest, outside of his residence. Subterfuge to gain access into the residence in order to make an arrest is not permitted.

THE ARREST

Keep in mind the statement "You're under arrest" doesn't have to be uttered the very moment you have established probable cause to arrest and intend to make the arrest. It is very foolish to tell someone "whacked out" on PCP that he is under arrest and *then* try to handcuff him.

In general, the suspect need not be advised that he is under arrest when he is actually engaged in the commission of the crime or when he is being pursued immediately after its commission. Most proactive "street" arrests occur under these circumstances, so hold the speech until the suspect is safely in custody.

MIRANDA

While we are on the subject of speeches, Miranda admonishments should not be shouted breathlessly into the face of the suspect as he lies exhausted at your feet. This is "TV law." There are three criteria to be met when an admonishment is to be given: the suspect is in police custody (not free to leave), the suspect is the focus of a criminal investigation, and the questions asked focus on this investigation.

These standards mean a suspect being interviewed *over the phone* does *not* have to be admonished, a witness not yet a suspect does *not* have to be admonished, and a suspect questioned about his identity does *not* have to be admonished.

I will avoid going into an in-depth discussion of suspect interrogation due to the prevalence of authoritative texts on the subject. However, there are a number of "street" techniques that should be mentioned. First, at some point, admonish everyone you arrest (keeping in mind your own department's policy). Especially admonish the ones you expect not to talk. You might be surprised by a positive response—and if they lie, it may be as useful as a confession.

For example, suppose you arrest a subject for possession of heroin. After the first hour you know the suspect is not going to know anything about the dope found in his pocket. In fact, he is probably going to tell you they are not his pants and he has never seen heroin before. A statement like this can be just as useful as a confession. At trial he will first have to convince a jury the pants were not his. And as far as the knowledge of heroin, a prior conviction for possessing heroin will destroy this lie.

But even more important is the valuable practice you will gain in addressing a hostile individual with your Miranda card and effectively delivering the speech in the face of the withering glare of a 38-year-old convict/junkie/robber. A training officer could not devise a more trying audience. The practice you get in voice control, mannerism, timing, and so on is invaluable when the time comes to admonish the child molester or rape suspect.

Admonishing a suspect is akin to performing stand-up comedy at the Dew Drop Inn, where the audience is disarmed before entering but the centerpieces are ripe vegetables. Timing and delivery are critical. Suspects are watching every move you make. One slip in your self-confidence and feigned nonchalance, the mental warning flags will go up, and suddenly he'll remember the "L.A. Law" episode that said a suspect should keep his mouth shut at all times.

So when do you admonish? At the point when you establish a "rapport." Ideally, during the rapport-building process, you have actually debriefed the suspect on the case at hand. For example, you were involved in a high-speed pursuit with the suspect but you're not sure after the foot chase if he was the driver or if suspect number two was the driver. Since this fact is essential to the auto-theft charge, you are looking for an admission that he was driving. You start to probe by suggesting he was pretty lame in hitting the telephone pole. You say it in a challenging manner, to get his competitive juices going.

Now the suspect is fairly sophisticated and knows what you are after, but he also thinks you can't use his statements against him until he is admonished. So he joins in this friendly banter, and you get your unadmonished admission. You write his statement into the report. At trial, of course, you are not allowed to bring the statement up. However, he foolishly takes the stand and denies driving the car. Well, our justice system frowns on such blatant lies, so his original statement is now brought in to impeach him (show he is a liar). The most likely course of events in this story is that his defense attorney will have read the statement and accepted a plea bargain or, at least, will not have allowed him to testify. Without his testimony the statement still cannot be brought up, but the jury will be left wondering why the suspect didn't get up there to deny driving.

If this suspect is not sophisticated or is simply predisposed to confessing, this "softening" or debriefing will ease the transition when you bring out the Miranda card. He is comfortable talking to you and comfortable talking about the incident. This is where the aforementioned practice pays off. The suspect will be watching you like a pit bull eyes a mailman. Your facial expression, hand movements, and voice must maintain the easygoing demeanor you had during the casual conversation. You have got to be smooth. Practice is the way to gain the experience needed to achieve this.

Street Tip: Have a second officer conduct the inter-

view—one who was not involved in the arrest. Thoroughly brief him on the facts of the case so he can detect a lie, and tell him what information you

are looking for. Often a suspect's pride will not allow him to admit wrongdoing to the officer who outran him, outdrove him, or outsmarted him.

FORCED CHEMICAL SAMPLES

An officer is allowed to use reasonable force to obtain a chemical sample (blood, breath, or urine) from a suspect if the sample is evidence. It may be a breath sample from a drunk driver, a urine sample from someone arrested for being under the influence of heroin, or a blood sample from a rape suspect for DNA matching. In any of the above circumstances, the force used must be reasonable and must not shock the conscience of the court.

It is not practical to force a sample of any body fluid except blood. To avoid "shocking the conscience," use physical restraints and have a suitable number of officers standing by to prevent movement. This method will reduce the likelihood of the suspect being injured during the blood draw. Once they see you are prepared to force a sample, suspects will submit to the withdrawal 99 percent of the time.

The importance of obtaining a sample on every single driving-under-the-influence or being-under-the-influence arrest must be emphasized. Without a chemical sample, the suspect's condition boils down to his word against the officer's. A positive chemical sample eliminates a multitude of effective defenses and forces "cop-outs" in a majority of cases. Don't ever book without a sample.

Street Tip: If you have a urine sample refusal from a junkie, put on a show for a forced draw. Junkies often have poor veins. Blood draws from them can be difficult ("shock the conscience"). These guys are "hard core" but they hate needles. That's right—they hate needles. A typical blood-draw needle is about 18 gauge, large for a needle. A junkie usually uses a diabetic syringe with a small

26-gauge needle. A 26-gauge needle goes in practically painlessly when done right. An 18-gauge always hurts. Tell him that all the yelling and threatening he is doing isn't going to stop the draw. He probably will then supply the urine sample.

During your efforts to obtain a urine sample, a junkie may have a difficult time urinating—a side-effect of the drugs. Give him a substantial quantity of water prior to any attempt at getting a sample, then take care of routine business before getting the sample. Again, you want to avoid resorting to a blood sample (the last resort) until you have removed all obstacles to a urine sample.

This is not because a blood sample is less reliable; there are advantages and disadvantages to both. You want to avoid being left without an alternative if no blood can be drawn.

THE REPORT

Paperwork begins the moment you decide to get out of your car and do something, whether it's to foot-patrol Drug Alley or stop someone. Once the suspect is booked, the writing actually begins. The arrest report will be the DA's sole source of information on the facts of the case, so if it isn't in there, it didn't happen. When writing, your frame of mind should be that the issuing DA reading this report is looking for a reason to throw the case out. You probably thought they were on your side. Wrong; they are on their own side. This means that because of understaffing, any case that's not picture-perfect is going to get the boot.

So as you write, think like the DA reviewing the case and looking for a reason to throw it out. He will focus first on the "reasonable suspicion" issue, as will the defense attorney. In fact, a motion to dismiss for lack of proper cause for the stop is the number-one weapon in a defense attorney's arsenal, particularly for self-initiated narcotics arrests.

When you begin to place the chronology of events on

paper, be sure you are clear on the fact you saw the "littering," "jay walking," or other objective symptoms *before* you decided to "contact," "approach,"

"detain," or speak with the individual. Each of these words relay to the DA or defense attorney you intended to "stop" the individual. If this intent occurred before you established a reasonable suspicion, then the stop will be viewed as being illegal.

Street Tip: A way to avoid confusion as to when you formulated the intent to contact a suspect is to simply get out of your car and begin to foot-patrol the area. There is no reason why you cannot walk by, walk in the area of, or pass by individuals or vehicles on foot patrol. Then, when you smell the odor of burning marijuana from 3 feet away or see the fresh track marks and sleepy facial expressions, you can stop the individual. Be sure to include this chronology in your report. For example: "I was assigned to uniformed patrol in the area of Euclid and Logan. I parked my vehicle in Hubb's liquor store parking lot and began a foot patrol of the area. I passed within 3 to 4 feet of Mr. Sullivan. I smelled a distinct chemical odor of ether coming from Mr. Sullivan. I associated this odor with PCP use, having made numerous previous PCP arrests. I saw Mr. Sullivan had a blank stare on his face, and he seemed unaware of my presence. I then contacted Mr. Sullivan."

Writing a police report is like climbing a ladder—each rung has to be in place before you can proceed to the next. It's not difficult, but you have to think and plan ahead before you make your next move.

SUMMARY

1. Use minor criminal codes, city ordinances, and vehicle code violations to establish a reasonable suspicion for a stop.

2. Justify a pat-down by asking the suspect whether he has any type of weapons on his person.

3. Clarify the nature of a bulge by questioning the suspect.

4. Whether it's a field interview, a contact inside a residence, or a traffic stop, actively look for contraband, giving probable cause for a search.

5. A consent search is legal cause for a search, but be careful under what conditions it is obtained.

6. Telephonic search warrants are simple. Use them every chance you get to build confidence and expertise in them.

7. Use of search-and-seizure waivers should become commonplace. Familiarize yourself with local street criminals who have them.

8. If you arrest someone out of his house, you need an arrest warrant, exigent circumstances, a search-and-seizure waiver, or probable cause for the arrest which occurred after you entered the residence.

9. If a suspect is arrested during the commission of a crime, handcuff him before you advise him that he is under arrest.

10. Use phone interrogations to avoid Miranda requirements.

11. Write down all admonished and unadmonished statements.

12. Admonish and question everyone you arrest.

13. Obtain a chemical sample in all under-the-influence cases.

CHAPTER 2 EVERYONE LIES TO THE POLICE

THE LYING CITIZEN

Y ou receive a radio call on a noninjury traffic accident at 43rd Street and Dwight Avenue. Upon your arrival, you are approached by Mr. Mainstream. He is eager to tell his story and be on his way. He points to a young lady resembling Squeaky Fromme of the Charlie Manson clan and blames her careless driving for the accident.

He rapidly runs down the events leading to the collision. He had finished shopping at the local Safeway supermarket with his friends' young boy and had driven cautiously out onto 43rd Street. He was then suddenly struck from behind by Ms. Fromme. She had obviously changed lanes improperly behind Mr. Mainstream, he says, and was following too closely. He finishes up by mentioning he is a retired fire fighter—an obvious

attempt to appeal to your pro-emer-
gency-services bias.

Forty-third is a southbound, three-
lane, one-way street. The supermarket
parking lot has an exit which allows departing traffic to
enter 43rd Street southbound. Mr. Mainstream is claiming he entered the first and proper southbound lane. Ms.
Fromme, he claims, was in the second southbound lane,
and after he entered the proper lane she then unsafely
moved into his lane, hitting him in the rear. His story
doesn't conflict with the vehicle damage.

Ms. Fromme is leaning against her '67 VW bug in her
granny dress. Her shoulder-length hair hasn't been
washed in several days, and one look at her brings
Woodstock to mind immediately. She is shaking as if a
cold wind were blowing through the thin material of her
flower-child dress. Ms. Fromme is obviously an "alter-
nate life-style" person.

The look in her eyes as you approach is one of total
intimidation. The closest she has ever been to the police
is her 15-inch Sony. You recall the first traffic accident
you had been involved in at 16 and the fear you felt. You
are Mr. Tact. Gently, you introduce yourself and ask
what happened.

Her story is Mr. Mainstream had left the parking lot as
described but entered the *second* southbound lane and
not the first. That's when the accident occurred. One
look at those misty eyes tells you she is telling the truth.

By this time, Mr. Mainstream has moved in close to
hear her story, and now Mr. Mainstream becomes Mr.
Intimidation. His years in public service provide him
with the ammunition he tries to use to berate her, dis-
credit her story and her appearance, and convince you
that you had better side with him. Maintaining your
cool, you decide to become Ms. Fromme's white knight.
This bully is not going to intimidate you or her into altering the conclusions of the accident report.

You examine the traffic lanes carefully for debris indicating a point of impact. No evidence of the collision is
visible on the asphalt. You glance around for possible
witnesses. An 11-year-old boy has been standing beside

"the Intimidator's" car, and you approach him. Mr. Mainstream moves into an intercept path, declaring the boy has nothing to say. "I'll decide that for myself," you respond, in your don't-mess-with-me voice.

You move out of earshot of the Intimidator and ask the boy who he is. The boy, Joey, is the son of Mr. Mainstream's best friend. Not a good sign. You then ask if he has heard the Intimidator's story, and he says he has. You ask if he knows it's wrong to tell a lie and that regardless of Mr. Mainstream's friendship with his father that he should tell the truth. He says he understands. You then ask the critical question, "What lane was he in?" Joey says the second lane. He describes the accident just as Ms. Fromme did.

You know from experience that a man like Mr. Mainstream or his attorney will immediately attack this boy's story, so you are going to be very precise in verifying it. You have Joey walk the exact path their car took, from the parking lot exit to the second lane. Joey shows no hesitation in retracing the path of the Intimidator's car into lane two.

Mr. Mainstream is now beside himself with anger. Ms. Fromme has a smile and a face that indicates she's thinking maybe all police officers aren't tools of the establishment.

Patrol officers should be careful in dealing with citizens, whether taking an accident report or responding to a routine radio call in a neighborhood dispute. Everyone has a private agenda regarding the way they live and the disputes they become involved in. Jealousy, anger, and spite are powerful emotions and will often taint an individual's version of an incident.

Be careful in accepting the reporting parties' versions of the facts. The old cliché that there are two sides to every story plays a prominent role here. Draw no conclusions and never make a statement of commitment until you have met and talked with the other side. And recognize that distortions of the truth may not always be intentional, but rather the result of imprecise perceptions and emotion.

THE LYING VICTIM

You're a rookie officer, and you respond to a call to take a report from a young lady regarding an attack from the previous night. You sit there taking notes like a large-mouth bass sucking in a plastic worm. You don't have a clue as to what is happening. As soon as you step outside the residence, your training officer tells you the case is bogus and explains why. He points out the contradictions in her statements and the implausibility of her story. The lesson is eye-opening: victims are not always truthful, so be careful when evaluating their stories.

You don't forget the lesson, and you now have about two years of experience as a patrol officer. You receive a call on a residential robbery. It's in a middle-class neighborhood, and residential robberies are unheard of there. The victim is a male in his early thirties. He tells you three to four males forced their way into his house, held him down, and then whipped him with an electrical cord. He has 20 to 25 red welts across his back.

The suspects didn't take or demand anything, so you rule out a drug rip-off or residential robbery. During the interview with the "victim," you notice the wife is somewhat detached from the events. You decide to take her aside and question her. She tells you they had had a fight earlier in the evening and that she left before the attack. She says she returned just before the police arrived.

Your finely tuned cerebral lie detector goes off. You start to evaluate the facts. Residential robberies are unusual in this area and not likely since nothing was taken. A whipping for no apparent reason? Who has something to gain from it? A family fight occurred just prior to the unwitnessed attack. You conclude that the "victim" staged the attack. Intense questioning of the "victim" follows, highlighting these discrepancies. He confesses.

Just as in the first incident, this victim was using the police to get attention and sympathy from a relative, much like people who attempt suicide. If common sense or the facts tell you to question the story, probe a little deeper.

Isolate witnesses for questioning, check
the victim's background, or look for
possible motivations, such as revenge,
attention or fear of punishment.

The lying "victim" is an interesting phenomenon
because most new officers are not prepared to have
someone lie to them. It never occurs to them that someone who wishes for police assistance would lie to those
who are there to help.

Criminals, witnesses, Joe Citizen, and even victims lie
to police. Accept this premise, and not only will you be
less likely to be conned, you'll be in a position to use the
lies to your advantage.

THE LYING CRIMINAL

For obvious reasons, criminals lie. They lie to avoid
arrest and confinement. Their lies focus on their involvement and their identities (see Chapter 3). Do not accept
at face value anything they have to say.

Hard-core criminals often are involved in more than
one type of scam. Avoid narrowing your focus in a criminal investigation to the obvious violation. Look for evidence of other less-visible criminal activity that they
may cover up with a lie.

For example, you arrest a junkie for a narcotics violation, and he describes his companion as his "girlfriend."
In reality, the "girlfriend" is a 16-year-old runaway/pros-
titute. Questioning his description of the relationship,
you separate the two. You interview the young girl and
develop probable cause to charge the junkie/pimp with
pandering and child endangerment.

While interviewing, be prepared to record any statements a suspect may make. This means writing the statements down at the moment they are made. Lying is hard
work, and even the best criminals get lazy or make mistakes. You must be prepared to catch mistakes by identifying changes in statements over time. Having recorded
conflicting statements prepares you to confront the subject with the inconsistencies when the time is right.

A second reason to record anything a suspect says is

that an ill-prepared lie is an effective way to impeach a suspect's testimony at trial. A prosecuting attorney will then be on notice as to the defendant's story and thus be in a position to destroy his credibility or leverage a plea bargain. A hint: even unadmonished responses may, at certain times, be used to impeach, so record all statements.

Remember that the individuals being addressed are professional criminals; they lie for a living. Some of these people are so persuasive in their lies that they seem to have convinced themselves they are innocent. The burden is on you to convince them the truth is the only chance they have in mitigating the trouble they are in. You can best sway their hard-core mentality by showing them that you are not fooled and are steadfast in your belief regarding their guilt. The following is an example of a unique persuasive technique.

You have arrested two juveniles for residential burglary and have transported them back to the crime scene. You are looking for a confession out of the two. In order to persuade them to confess, you must convince them you have substantial evidence to establish their guilt. However, there are no eyewitnesses to the burglary, and your physical evidence (shoe prints in front and backyard) is not yet conclusive as to their guilt. You are going to have to come up with something unique to persuade them to confess.

Your suspects, Mr. Cookson and Mr. Crotz, are 17 and fairly sophisticated. They are street-smart but not yet hard-core. The first item of business is to separate the two. It's much easier to eat a hogey when it's cut in two, and it's much easier to gain a confession when suspects are separated. Cookson goes into a different squad car parked in front of the victim's residence, and Crotz stays in yours. Both have a clear view of the victim's front yard. You now remove both their pairs of shoes.

You've established a rapport with Crotz, so you'll work on him first. Once he has confessed you'll use his confession to persuade Cookson to confess.

You start with the shoe prints in the front yard. You

make a production of protecting the prints (cardboard box), measuring them, and then photographing them.

The next step is the examination of the suspects' shoes. Both patterns obviously match the ones in the yard, but you're going to make a media event out of it. You focus your police car's spotlight on the front-yard shoe prints. You then hold the shoes up in the glare. You and the reporting officer break into wide grins and pat each other on the back.

Now for the finale. You walk confidently over to your car and whip open the door. You throw the shoes on the car's floorboard and give Mr. Crotz that know-it-all look every teacher and supervisor you have ever had hates. Mr. Crotz wilts like a prom queen at 3 A.M.

He blurts out, "It was Cookson's idea. I didn't even go inside." Your cheeks hurt as you attempt to keep from smiling. You don't want him to suspect you ever doubted their guilt. You ask where the stolen property is, and he tells you it is at his house. Confronted with Mr. Crotz's confession, Mr. Cookson eventually acknowledges his guilt. Both are charged with burglary and conspiracy to commit burglary.

Setting the stage for interrogation is as important as the interrogation itself. Suspects have myriad reasons to confess. You want to be sure you have done nothing to prevent this predisposition to confess.

By laying the physical evidence out for both suspects to observe and consider, the officer makes his argument without words or accusations. He does not place his ego or the suspects on the line. Without these obstacles to confession, the suspects were in a position to follow their own selfish predisposition to confess. An officer's abrasive or condescending attitude is often the biggest barrier to obtaining a statement or confession. Be smart and eliminate this needless barrier through tact and strategy.

Street Tip: Questions directed at suspects should be phrased so that they elicit a response that the suspects think will exonerate them but that will actually implicate them in the crime at hand.

Example one: You have arrested a drug dealer and you are looking for a statement acknowledging the drugs are possessed for sale and not just personal use.

Officer: You don't sell drugs to kids do you—just your friends, right?

Suspect: That's right, just my friends; I would never sell to kids.

Example two: You have a suspect in custody for robbery, and you are looking for statement acknowledging his intent to steal.

Officer: Now, when you went into the store you weren't getting money for beer and a card game; you needed money to feed your kids, right?

Suspect: That's right, my kids needed to eat.

An additional tack in interrogating criminal suspects is to keep them talking. Once they begin to converse with you, keep the conversation going. The longer they talk the quicker their guard will drop. Either they will be relaxed enough to reveal the truth, or they will slip and say something they didn't intend to reveal.

Even if what they are saying is a lie, the more they talk the more intricate the lie becomes. An intricate lie is harder to remember and easily attacked with proven facts.

To keep the conversation moving and thus more casual, prepare conversation and questions to ask as he is talking. Don't allow a gap in the talk to occur. If you are stymied for words, revert back to identifying questions or conversation related to the business at hand (does he want his car impounded or left at the scene, does he need to take something with him, whom does he wish to call?). This will give you time to generate additional questions without appearing to force it.

THE LYING WITNESS

For less obvious but equally understandable reasons, witnesses lie to the police. They lie about who they are (fear of an outstanding arrest warrant), what they say (they don't want to get involved), or who did it (friend, relative, or homeboy). Depending on the circumstances, it may be critical for you to receive truthful information from a witness.

The most common lying witness is one to a gang-related criminal act, such as a drive-by shooting, assault, or murder. Witnesses affiliated with a gang either through their own membership or their boyfriends' will know who committed the assault. Through the gang and community grapevine, as well as personal observation, these people will know the name of the attacking gang and quite possibly the identity of the shooter.

Interviewing witnesses in front of their "homeboys" will be useless. Separate each witness from the crowd both physically and visually. Talking to the police is prohibited, regardless of the motivation. Explain to them their identity will be protected, that you will be talking to a large number of people and no one will know who spoke up. Often your witness is not a hard-core gang member but an associate not as antipolice as others but still under social pressure to conform to the code of silence. Isolating witnesses from this pressure will give you the best chance of breaking through the code by appealing to their own suppressed sense of right and wrong.

Verify the information you get and if it is a lie, try to determine why. If it's because of a minor warrant reassure the witness there are other ways to handle a warrant than by arrest (reschedule an appearance date, post bail, "work it off," etc.).

As troubling as this sounds, never accept what people say as the unqualified truth, no matter what their positions in the situation. Always be skeptical of their stories, but silently so. If you are provided with facts that can be verified independently, such as identities or alibis, check them out. If deceit is discovered, gather all the facts necessary to convince the person you know the whole truth. *Then* approach the person and ask for an explanation or the truth. Don't be confrontational or accusatory. They will clam up, and you won't get anywhere. Express concern regarding the conflicts and ask them to offer an explanation. This leaves the person with an "honorable" out.

There is always time to be hard-nosed; save that as your last resort.

SUMMARY

1. Don't accept anyone's version of the events without verification.

2. Write down statements at the time they are made.

3. Keep suspects talking.

4. Verify witness statements with the facts and with other witness statements.

5. Separate witnesses before and during an interview.

6. Don't be accusatory. Simply ask for an explanation of any discrepancies in victim, witness, and suspect statements.

oday is a routine day, and you're on your beat paying courtesy calls to the local drug dealers. It's a slow morning, but by the fourth house you have company. Judy is sitting in the driver's seat of a '57 Chevy pick-up truck parked around the corner from a house on your list. The registration on the vehicle is out of date, providing you with cause to stop her. You approach the truck and contact Judy.

The first thing you notice is "tracks" over veins on the back of her hands. Tracks are the scar tissue which result from the repeated injection of illegal drugs. Scar tissue develops because of impurities in the drugs, the use of dull and unclean needles, and failure to clean the skin prior to injection.

She states she doesn't have any identification, but a junkie without identification is a junkie with a warrant.

rant. This is a hard-core philosophy but one that has passed the test of hundreds of drug arrests.

Your legal position at this time supports the detention of Judy for a period of two hours while you attempt to verify her name. The vehicle code allows such a detention prior to releasing a subject on a promise to appear. You spend the two hours working every computer file, including phone numbers, license plate, past and present addresses, Social Security number, criminal history, and so on, but no luck. Time's up, and she must be released.

She is good. She's a good liar, accommodating and courteous. But it doesn't make any difference. You've been had. Well, maybe not. You did walk away from the contact with her photograph. But whom do you show it to?

Mentally, you run through the evidence you have. Judy is in her early thirties with a sizable heroin problem. By the length of her tracks, her age, and her attitude, she has been shooting dope for many years. That means she has been arrested numerous times and has had extensive contact with the police.

She stated she grew up in a nearby city. Your current location is about half a mile from that city's limits. With your belief in Judy's criminal past, you figure one of the local officers must know her.

You drive the five miles to their police station and start to show the picture around. She is immediately recognized as Linda Woods. A warrant check reveals a no-bail burglary warrant.

So where is she now? You hit the computer again and find the most recent of the six addresses under her name. The address is six months old and an apartment, so you know it's a shot in the dark due to the transiency of addicts.

You wait until the next morning and enlist the assistance of a fellow officer. You have the officer knock on the door because you know if she sees you she won't answer. Ms. Woods answers the door, and you pop out from around the corner. Her mouth drops open, and she looks like she just heard the jail-house door clanging shut.

The purpose of this chapter is to assist an officer in identifying a suspect who has lied about his or her identity. The following list contains several rules that should be followed every time you engage in the "game":

1. Verify everyone's identity prior to release on a citation, field interview, or jail booking. Verification may be as easy as asking a companion for the suspect's name or making a phone call to a residence. A subject without *any* identification is suspect. Be especially diligent in verifying identity.

2. Make sure your knowledge of search-and-seizure laws is up-to-date. Portions of the game include a physical search for identification and a detention of the suspect. Your best approach in handling an unidentified subject is to place him under arrest for any offense: traffic, city ordinance, misdemeanor, or felony. This includes minor offenses, such as littering, dog off leash, no driver's license, etc. An arrest based on proper probable cause, no matter how minor, provides some protection for an officer later accused of improper behavior.

3. The criminal lies for a reason, almost always because of a warrant or belief that one exists. Rarely do criminals lie to avoid the present arrest. An exception may be an ex-con type looking at some serious time behind the arrest.

Criminals generally "live for the moment." Knowing they have a warrant and will most likely be denied an O.R. (release on own recognizance) because of it, they lie to avoid the consequences of the warrant, not the present arrest.

Exceptions to the above are juveniles and minors with alcohol. Juveniles will lie about their identity to avoid the wrath of their parents. Minors with alcohol will lie about their age. If you suspect someone is underage, ask about it, and if the response is "21," be on guard. Because 21 is the least adult age they are willing to risk impersonating, minors with alcohol are always 21, never any older.

Remember, most crooks have a better understanding

of the courts and jails than you do. They know once booked, they will generally be released quickly due to overcrowding. Attempting to avoid the consequences of the present situation is unimportant because of this quick release. So, *always* focus on finding *the* warrant. If an initial warrant check under what you now believe is a proper name is negative, keep looking. Double and triple check the "new" name. Be sure to check all available warrant systems under *all* of his names, including local systems, National Crime Information Center (NCIC), and parole.

An officer should be careful in allowing another officer or dispatcher to run the warrant check. Very often there is a miscommunication in the spelling of the suspect's name or what exactly you are looking for. If you want it done right, do it yourself.

4. If you have contacted an individual with prison tattoos and/or tracks with no record, the suspect is lying. Start the game. This is the person the plan was designed for.

5. A subject without a middle name is probably lying. Follow the listed steps for proper identification.

6. If it turns out your subject is a parolee, be sure to contact his parole officer to get a parole hold on him. This prevents the suspect from being released after a couple of hours and allows the parole officer time to revoke parole.

THE PROCESS

What follows is the step-by-step outline of the game. Remember, if you don't establish the suspect's identity prior to booking, it may never happen.

1. Upon initial contact, write down the subject's complete identifying information, preferably on a field interrogation form, with or without identification. This is important for several reasons:

• You won't remember everything the suspect has told you.

- The suspect won't remember everything he said.
- The suspect will change the information later.

The key to identifying "John Doe" is to find a kernel of truth in what has been said. Your investigation will focus on this piece of truth. A criminal will not lie about everything; it takes too much effort to remember all the lies. If the suspect thinks you are fooled with a bad name, other information may be accurate. However, as time goes by and you probe deeper into the suspect's identity, his guard will go up and this kernel of truth may evaporate. That's why it is critical to write statements down at the onset, particularly Social Security numbers and addresses.

2. Be very specific when questioning the suspect as to identifying information. If the question is regarding his address, be sure to get the exact numbers, including the apartment number. Ask for his last previous address at this time. Often the second address turns out to be his true address or the key to his identity. Suspects are caught off guard with this question. They will be prepared to give one false address, but not two.

Phrase questions in a manner requiring more than a yes or no answer. Ask *when* he was last arrested, not *if* he has been arrested before. Ask *which state* his driver's license is from, not *if* he has one.

Have the suspect spell his whole name. Difficulty in spelling it is evidence he is lying to you. This may be enough to establish probable cause for his arrest and entitle you to search him for identification. A correctly spelled name is also critical in computer checks. Do not assume the name has a common spelling.

Ask the suspect what his horoscope sign is. If it doesn't match, you have further evidence he is lying.

3. After you have established proper cause for a search by obtaining consent or establishing probable cause, search him for identification and paperwork. Often cleaning receipts, sales slips, and letters will pro-

vide adequate documentation of identity. Even hard-core criminals do not lie about their names during day-to-day activity. The majority are prepared to lie to a police officer but not to a store clerk. Examine the backs of family photographs for the names of the people depicted as well as the name of the person the photo was given to.

4. Locate the subject's vehicle and/or car keys. If he identifies a vehicle as his, check it for identification and make note of the vehicle identification number (VIN) and the license plate number. If he denies ownership of a vehicle and has car keys, check the keys against vehicles in the immediate vicinity.

5. Separate the John Doe from companions before starting the game; you don't want *them* putting their guard up. Ask the companions what his name is. Do not offer the bad name given to you. The most common response is a first name or a nickname. Often you can check the nickname through your computer system. If the first name is different from what Doe gave you, this may be enough to arrest him for lying to you or even enough for correct identification. Be sure to identify the companions adequately. Their identities may provide a lead as to Doe's.

6. Examine the subject for tattoos, particularly word or letter tattoos. These are almost as good at identifying people as serial numbers are in identifying property. Remember, when making arrests take time to note any tattoos a suspect has, as this could play a key role in his arrest later.

7. After the suspect is under arrest, transport him to the reported residence. If he is feigning cooperation, you may be able to obtain a consent search of the house for identification. Oftentimes he has forgotten about some contraband he has in the house. Be sure to check with neighbors as to his identity. Preface the inquiry with,

"Before we let him go, we need some- **41**
one to help identify him." Do not say, THE NAME GAME
"He's lying to us." This will alienate
most people immediately.

COMPUTER CHECKS

If the above steps prove unsuccessful or you still want
to verify a name, the following are computer checks listed
in order from the most successful to least successful. Be
careful in the spelling of suspects' names. Computers are
very quirky on checking "near misses," so have the suspect
spell his name for you. If he has difficulty spelling it, this
adds evidence to charges of false impersonation or lying to
the police. Double check with female suspects to make sure
you have both their maiden and married names.

1. Run the name through standard criminal history
files. Keep in mind someone with only a few previous
arrests may still be lying about his name. He may simply
have succeeded in lying to other officers about his name.
Do not use this short criminal history as an identity verification. If there is an arrest record on file for the name your
suspect has given you, pull a copy of the booking photo
and the fingerprints on file and do a comparison. Be particularly careful about relying solely on the booking
photo; relatives with similar physical features often inter-
change names. Use the fingerprint comparison to be sure.
Younger criminals, juveniles, and those up to 20 are
ineffective liars. Their criminal histories will usually
contain their true names. The older the criminal, the
more experienced and the more successful he becomes
in lying about identity. Tracing a suspect's criminal history back to his teens is a good identity verification.
An older suspect does not all of a sudden become a
criminal. Criminal history most often started in high
school. A criminal history that suddenly begins when a
suspect is in his mid-twenties is suspect. Keep looking
for the trail of arrests that goes back to the younger years.

2. Address checks are often the most successful com-

puter checks. Ask for both present and past addresses. The criminal doesn't necessarily always lie to the police, usually only when there is a warrant outstanding. This is one of the "kernels of truth." A prior arrest or citation with the same address may return with the suspect's true identity.

Social Security number checks are often successful, even if you are given the wrong number. The wrong number may connect you to a previous arrest with a true identity. Even if you are given an incorrect number, running a partial number (the first and second sets of digits) may provide you with a range of possibilities. To narrow those possibilities, run the partial number with sex and race identifiers.

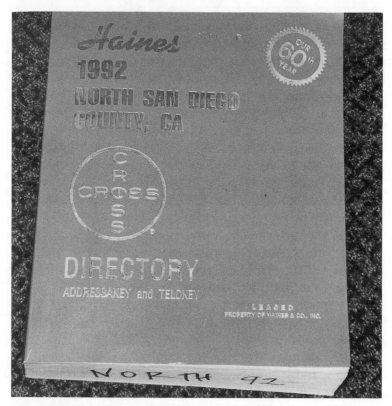

Phone numbers found in the possession of an unidentified suspect may be checked through a "backwards" directory.

3. Contact your Crime Analysis Unit to assist you with the more time-consuming checks, such as tattoo checks. They may offer you some hints and can be conducting checks while you process the prisoner.

4. Run a computer check of phone numbers in the suspect's possession or numbers you obtained through the computer or a backwards directory. (Also called a criss-cross directory, this program lists phone numbers in numerical order with corresponding addresses It is available at most police departments and in public libraries.) Call the numbers and ask for the parents. Parents are less likely to lie than siblings.

5. After the initial interview with the prisoner, explain the situation: you need to verify identity prior to a release on a cite or field interview. Ask for an address or phone number where identity can be verified. Tell the suspect he is lying and is not going anywhere until identified. It may be that the suspect is getting tired of the repeated questioning and and is beginning to worry about missing out on a hot jailhouse dinner. (Hard-core criminals are very conscious of mealtimes in local jails. They often prefer a good meal over freedom. To them, an arrest is often just a nuisance since they will most likely spend only a few days or a couple of hours in jail. If they're tired of playing the name game, they will just as soon be booked in to jail and then get fed and released as it is to sit in the backseat of your patrol car. Use this argument to persuade them to tell you who they are.)

6. Book the suspect into jail as a "John Doe." Jails are overcrowded and understaffed; there may be minimal, if any, attempt to verify identity. However, if the jail has a policy of not releasing Does or delaying Doe releases, the suspect may elect to confess to avoid processing delays.

7. Depending on your agency's computer capabilities, you may be able to run a computerized fingerprint check. In the state of California, there is the CAL-ID sys-

tem. This system is capable of running developed latent prints and fingerprint cards and can even read prints off the bare hand. Its data base consists of subjects arrested and fingerprinted throughout California.

8. After booking, and as manpower and personal work ethics dictate, walk a photo around the neighborhood you found him in. You may get lucky, and sometimes that's the name of the game.

There are several skills to be gained through repeated exposure to this game. The most important is the ability to detect the liar. On the surface, an officer well adapted to the game appears to have developed an instinct for determining who is lying. A closer examination shows the officer does not have an innate, ambiguous ability to detect liars but a well-developed sense for picking up on the small clues given off by the John Doe.

OFFICER	DOE
"What's your name?"	"Who, me? May name is John Doe." (Lengthy answer gives time for false response.)
"What's your date of birth?"	"July 13, 1956, ah . . . 1957." (Year is most often off by one or two years.)
"How old are you?"	"Twenty-five, ah . . . twenty-six." (Won't match date of birth.)
"Do you have any I.D.?"	"No, left it at home (lost it, it was stolen)." (Doe anticipated contact with the police.)

These answers are indicators that the game has started. Don't let on that you feel the suspect is lying. Acquire as much information as possible before he puts his guard up.

The key to the "game" is the willingness to go the extra step and take time to make that computer check or phone call.

SUMMARY

1. Verify everyone's identity prior to release.
2. Always look for an arrest warrant.
3. Run your computer checks yourself.
4. Notify parole officers of contacts with parolees.
5. Focus computer searches on a known truth in the suspect's statements.
6. Address checks are usually the most successful computer checks.
7. Write the suspect's initial identifying information down.
8. Search suspects and their cars for identifying paperwork, including sales receipts, photographs, and letters.
9. Have the suspect spell his whole name.
10. Question multiple suspects separately.
11. Examine all tattoos closely.
12. Call phone numbers found in the suspect's possession.

CHAPTER 4 MAN-TRACKING TECHNIQUES—THE ART OF THE FOOT PURSUIT

O ver the radio, you hear a broadcast of a residential burglary that just occurred. The burglary was interrupted by a witness, and there are two suspects. One has fled in a nondescript blue car, and the other escaped on foot. The location is 10 miles away, and three units are responding. You make a mental note of the call but stay on your beat.

Twenty minutes later, a call goes out about a prowler now three blocks from the burglary call. You know who it is: suspect number two. He's on foot, his ride is history, and the first units have "run him to ground," but they don't know it. Here's your chance for an easy one.

You've been through the scenario before: loud cars, loud radios, and noisy cops announce their presence. The suspect dives for the bushes and waits for the circus to clear out. You know you don't have long to wait because cops have almost as short an attention span as 2-year-olds. It takes you 15 minutes to get there and another 15 for the officers doing the "grid search" to break it down and head for easier pickings.

Flashback time, 0530 hours. It's cold, it's dark, you're tired, but hey, you're 13, you've got a .22, and it's time to kill Thumper. There's nothing you can do about it; it's as if God said, "ALL 13-YEAR-OLD BOYS WILL KILL RAB-BITS." So you go with the flow and head to your favorite hunting ground.

After a few trips to the backcounty, on less-than-legal hunting expeditions, you've learned a few tricks. First, go for the high ground. The reason is simple: you can see more rabbits, more rabbit trails, and more sheriff's deputies.

Second, rabbits are quick, but not smart. (Maybe that's why cops call fleeing suspects "rabbits.") Rabbits are ter-ritorial and rarely stray far from home. They run in cir-cles along delineated trails. After a short distance, they stop and wait for "Opie with a gun" to walk on by. Not too bad of a plan, except for two things: one, they have the "If I close my eyes they can't see me" attitude, and two, they are impatient. So, if they happen to stop in a clear area or if you wait long enough, they will move. Either way they're in trouble.

The same occurs with criminals. They're impatient and are just waiting for the cops to leave. Once the loud police cars and noisy cops leave, the criminal will make his move to escape.

Back to the story. You take the high ground, a street over-looking the house where the prowler was last seen. Forty-five minutes later, up pops the burglar from behind a fence.

The key to tracking a criminal suspect on foot is understanding his frame of mind, motivation, and physi-cal condition. In a foot chase or even a stale hunt, the criminal is after two things: to avoid arrest at all costs and to get home.

AVOID THE CHASE

It is important to note some preventative measures

which may reduce the number of foot pursuits you have to engage in. The simplest is to place a detainee in your police car during the contact.

Whether the stop is a routine field interview or an investigation of some crime, the subject is being detained. He is not free to leave. Being placed in your patrol car's backseat is no more of a detention than if you were to have him stand on the sidewalk next to you.

Most patrol cars have some type of shield or barrier between the driver's compartment and the passenger compartment, hence the term "cage car."

These vehicles are roving jail cells and should be used as such. Of course, pat the suspect down for weapons prior to placing anyone in the car.

Be aware, however, that the use of force or physical restraints may elevate a detention into an arrest. Handcuffing a detained individual may elevate the stop to an arrest. Be sure to have probable cause established

Placing a detainee behind a police car's cage circumvents flight, fights, and hassles—use it.

for such an arrest if you elect to handcuff a suspect.

The advantages to having him secure
in your vehicle are numerous. The most
obvious is that it prevents an attempt to flee upon receiving
notice of a warrant. There will be no fight or chase. If an
unruly crowd develops, you simply drive away.

Once you decide to make an arrest and handcuffing is
necessary, be sure to do it in a safe location free of friends
and relatives. Open the door with the appropriate number of officers at the ready. Direct the suspect to turn
sideways on the seat, and handcuff him while he's in a
seated position.

You should be aware of the warning signs given off by
a suspect inclined to run. Suspects looking to flee get
what are called "rabbit eyes." They look from side to side,
evaluating the best path of escape. There is no eye contact. They often slowly take a step back from you just
before the mad dash for freedom. Once you observe these
behaviors in a suspect, take him into physical custody
immediately. He is just a split second away from running,
and this will be your first and safest chance for control.

THE BEGINNING OF THE CHASE

The key factors determining the escape method are the
physical layout of the land and the physical condition of
the suspect. Although most patrol officers have run across
the human gazelle in foot chases, most criminals are in
average to poor physical condition. A foot pursuit of any
length will usually result in their immediate collapse. The
weighed-down patrol officer in average police officer
shape is quite capable of capturing the suspect in a
straight pursuit. However, because the chase is at night
and/or through numerous backyards, the suspect may easily hide and wait out the deluge of noisy patrol officers.

ANIMAL-TRACKING TECHNIQUES

A patrol officer can do several things to locate such a
suspect. First, keep in mind that the escapee is exhaust-

ed. He has run as far as possible and is now looking to rest up. He will then attempt to make a stealthy escape through the perimeter set up by other

officers. Or he plans to "hole up" and wait the troops out.

With this in mind, you need to employ an animal-tracking technique that focuses on the last location spoor has been found. Spoor is evidence which indicates the presence of the animal, such as tracks, bent grass, or a spot of blood. In most foot chases, spoor is either the last glimpse or the last sound of the suspect going over a fence. However, it may also be dropped stolen property, an overturned trash can, or a barking dog.

In the heat of a foot pursuit or even in the approach to

Suspect's sweatshirt is inside out and dropped in a location that indicates he fled into the rear yard.

a stale scene, most officers continue to run or drive haphazardly in areas they suspect the criminal may have gone. Keep in mind that the suspect is tired and, although he evaded you initially, he is looking for a place to hide. Now focus on the area where he was last seen or heard.

Stealth is mandatory at this point. Put your walkie-talkie earplug in your ear, put your keys in your pocket, and stop waving your flashlight around aimlessly. At night, your hearing is your best sense. Focus on the sounds around you and identify them. Stand quietly at the suspect's last known location and listen for dogs barking, gates being opened, and fences being climbed.

Let your eyes adjust to the darkness and catch your breath. Then begin a slow, careful search of the immediate area. Quietly walk from that position to the path of least resistance (downhill), checking obvious hiding places. Like the rabbit, he is more than likely hiding out until the heat is off.

If the physical landscape affords you the opportunity, look into the distance for a likely goal of the suspect. It may be a school, shopping center, or vacant field. Now, visually work your way back to his last known location, looking for the path of least resistance.

The best way to visualize this technique is to recall the last time you were out hiking in the country. Whether your goal was a particular landmark or simply a shortcut to the car, you did the same thing. You fixed your car in your sights and then evaluated the easiest path through the stickers and barbed wire to get there. You may also have been conscious of not traveling a path that led to a dead end.

BLOOD TRAILS

Common in tracking criminals is the presence of a blood trail. Criminals often cut themselves in an assault or while forcing entry into a building. These may be serious enough to leave a visible, trackable blood trail. If the direction of travel is already known, then just focus on following the trail.

However, if direction of travel is not known, then a

close examination of the blood drops
is necessary. The narrow end of the
drop will usually indicate direction of
travel. Conflicting shapes may indicate

the cut is on an arm swinging back and forth. If this is the
case, use the animal-tracking techniques described in the
previous section to determine direction of travel.

The color of the blood will give a rough estimation of
elapsed time. Bright red indicates a recent deposit; the
darker it becomes, the more time has elapsed. A ghoulish
experiment to assist in estimating time is to take advantage of an accidental cut, comparing the changes in color
of your blood as time elapses.

If you do have a seriously cut suspect, be sure to notify local hospitals of the situation; the suspect will probably show up at an emergency room for treatment.

DIRECTION OF TRAVEL

Speculating on a suspect's direction of travel, look at
age. A suspect in a gang-related shooting will head in the
direction of home "turf." A white male in a black community will head for a white part of town. A juvenile
will follow neighborhood trails to his home, while an
adult may work his way on side streets to his parked
vehicle. All suspects will move to a location where they
can blend in and feel comfortable.

If you're fortunate enough to be in a position to take
the high ground, then do so. High ground provides the
visibility necessary to see in backyards, over fences, or
through to the next street. More than likely, the suspect
will have moved to the "low ground" simply because it's
easier to get to. As he moves, you may direct other officers to his location, as police helicopters often do, or you
may move on an intercept path.

Search for at least an hour. Most cops don't search for
longer than a half hour, either because they bore easily or
calls for service pull them out. Criminals know this and
get antsy themselves, so they also begin to move within
half an hour if the noise and lights of police helicopters
and patrol units have died down.

If you feel the immediate area has been checked well, then change the focus of the search. Your attention should now be on physical locations which may be an attraction to someone tired, thirsty, and looking for transportation. This includes pay phones at convenience stores, bus stops, shopping centers, and schools. Schools are particularly attractive to juveniles because of their familiarity with them. They know where to hide, where the phones are, and where the drinking fountains are.

If you spot a likely suspect, call in assistance. He has run once and will run again. Position your help to block any escape path. Approach in an indirect way and pre-

The high ground allows you to look into yards, locate escape routes, and determine possible destinations, such as shopping centers, convenience stores, and schools.

tend to focus your attention else-
where. Like the ostrich, a criminal
often pretends you don't exist and he
was not involved. He may feel no one

actually got his description and the police were only
chasing a ghost. Use this to your advantage on the
approach. Keep him off guard by calling out to someone
else or by pretending to be there for other reasons (e.g.,
making a phone call, shopping, investigating a traffic
accident, looking for a lost child). Once you're close
enough, position yourself to block the most likely avenue
of escape, then either use your most authoritative voice
or actually grab him to gain control. The method used
will be based on individual safety concerns.

Grabbing a very large individual after a tiring pursuit
may not be a good idea. He may either sense your weak-
ened state or simply attempt to muscle away. Try the
voice command first. He may be intimidated or tired
enough to comply.

Be careful drawing your gun and ordering a suspect to
freeze. If you actually intend to shoot a running suspect,
then that's fine. But more times than not an officer will
draw a gun in an attempt to intimidate the suspect into
giving up. The officer is tired and frustrated and hopes
the threat will bring the chase to an end. Sometimes it
does; sometimes it doesn't. Criminals are very aware of
police shooting policies and often will ignore such com-
mands. Now, you either shoot improperly or reholster
your weapon and start the chase all over again.

THE CAPTURE

Upon contacting the suspect, make note of physical
conditions. Take a photograph of him and seize his clothing as evidence. Look for any heavy breathing, perspiration, grass stains, torn clothing, mud on the shoes or
pants, dirty hands or clothing, or scratches on his body.
This evidence may be essential in establishing that he
was the one actually fleeing the crime scene.

Be cautious in interrogating the suspect immediately
after capture. Officers involved in foot pursuits, as well

as vehicle pursuits, have a high amount of adrenaline flowing through their systems and are generally not in a good mood. Immediately confronting the criminal in such an agitated state may have some unpleasant repercussions for the criminal. These events may build a barricade to any successful interrogation of the suspect later. Either turn the interrogation over to someone not emotionally involved or wait until you have rested, replenished body fluids, and changed into an untorn uniform.

During the interrogation, act as if there is no doubt in your mind that he is the suspect. Don't let him attempt to deny he was the subject being chased. If he won't admit to the crime involved, at the minimum have him

Retrace the path of a fleeing suspect to look for discarded weapons, drugs, and clothing.

acknowledge he was the one being chased from the start. Ask him whether he saw the pit bull in that one yard or how he scaled that fence

so quickly. Acknowledging these events indicates he was the one being chased. Fleeing from the police is called an "admission" and may be used against him to show "guilty knowledge" of the underlying offense.

THE WRAP-UP

Now that the chase is over, begin the search for narcotics, weapons, and clothing the suspect stashed during an escape attempt. The suspect probably will have disposed of such items either along the escape route or at a rest point. (While recovering, a suspect is thinking a little more clearly and may conceal evidence.) If you locate a resting place, check likely hiding spots. Pay close attention to any disturbed soil. Burying evidence is a habit picked up in prison exercise yards.

Hold on to any clothing he may have disposed of along the way. Suspects will usually discard shirts and jackets to alter their appearance. Such evidence may be critical in a later lineup, particularly a "curbstone" one.

Luck, physical conditioning, and persistence are the keys to a capture. At the scene, persistence is the only element over which you have control. Take time to get out of your car and employ the methods described. Continually applying little things is what results in quality arrests. That's the difference between a "street cop" and the average police officer.

SUMMARY

1. Use your cage car to secure a detainee.

2. Start your search in the area where the fleeing suspect was last seen or heard or evidence of his presence was found.

3. A suspect's escape route will generally take the path of least resistance, often downhill.

4. Use the high ground to search for the suspect and

a likely avenue of escape.

5. Search for at least an hour.

6. Once the immediate vicinity has been searched thoroughly, move your search to schools, shopping centers, and convenience stores.

7. Make note of the suspect's physical condition upon capture and photograph him.

8. Retrace the suspect's path of escape for evidence.

9. Solicit an admission he was the one being chased.

10. Consider having a second officer conduct the interrogation.

CHAPTER 5 AUTO THIEF APPREHENSION AND VEHICLE PURSUITS

alfway through your shift you take your midmorning 7-11 break (not an official lunch break, but one of several to keep the caffeine and sugar levels at an acceptable high). As you casually pull back into traffic, you notice a motorcycle rider stop at the light ahead. He is in the lane next to you as you pull up to the limit line. He knows you're there, but he is staring straight ahead as if in a trance.

The bike is a Kawasaki 1000, dark red with racing fairings and cafe-style handlebars. You have the same one parked in your garage.

Aside from his inanimate figure, you sense something inappropriate about the rider. You scan him from head to toe trying to understand the reasons behind your suspicions. Then it hits you—he is wearing a full-face Motocross helmet, yellow in color. Not only is this helmet designed for off-road motorcycle riding, but the helmet color doesn't match the bike. Not that you're Calvin Klein and think a person's attire has to be color-coordinated, including the helmet, but this helmet just doesn't "fit the picture."

You know this bike cost $6,980. The helmet is valued at $150. When a guy spends that much money on a "rice rocket," the dealer throws in a matching street helmet. That's good business, and that's what's wrong with the picture.

The light turns green, and you quickly memorize the small digits on the license plate. The bike rider immediately turns right onto a side street. The chase has started. You run the plate, and it comes back stolen. This guy's eyes are focused on his mirror, and as soon as you hit your overheads, the bike accelerates to double the speed of light. Fast bike, lousy rider; the first corner he hits is covered with overspray from Mrs. Johnson's sprinkler. Down he goes, and the chase is over.

PROFILING

Essential in the apprehension of auto thieves as well as a number of other criminals is the use of a "profile." A profile is a number of facts indicating a subject or car needs to be investigated further. For example, prison tattoos on the forearm of a suspect are indicative of a drug addict as well as a convict. These facts tell you to look for the objective symptoms of drug use and to establish parole status. The same line of reasoning applies to a set of facts attributable to a stolen car or auto thief.

The use of profiles by police officers is not only desirable but essential in the pursuit of the criminal element. Men in three-piece suits do not commit street crimes. Street criminals look like stereotypical criminals. They may be unkempt and have a hardened look about them, wear gang clothing, dress as the classic prostitute, or sport prison tattoos. This type of stereotyping or profiling is essential for a street cop's efficient use of time.

Using profiles allows an officer to place limited

resources in the areas most likely to
result in an arrest or prevent a crime.
The purpose of a profile is to narrow
your search from the hundreds of

autos you pass in a day to the 25 most likely to be stolen.

A word of caution on the use of profiles is necessary
at this point. A profile match is not probable cause for an
arrest, nor is it reasonable suspicion for a stop. It is, however, enough to focus your attention on a particular car.
You may then run the license plate to see if it's stolen or
examine the vehicle for equipment violations without
initiating a stop. Remember, profiling at this level does
not legally support any intrusion into a suspect's behavior. Legal cause—independent of the profile—must be
established before you take *any* action.

STOLEN VEHICLE PROFILE

A majority of stolen vehicles share common features.
Labeling these characteristics establishes the profile of a
stolen vehicle. This profile may vary from region to
region or from one part of a city to the next. The individual officer may apply the following general profile characteristics and then narrow the profile based on personal
experience.

Foreign-made automobiles—Toyotas, Nissans, and
Mazdas in particular—have a higher theft rate than vehicles built in America. A big reason for this is the fact the
steering column locking mechanisms on these vehicles
are easier to defeat than those on American-made vehicles. Often a simple straight-blade screwdriver is all that
is necessary to defeat the lock on a foreign car. The thief
places the blade of the screwdriver in the key slot and
then forces the ignition switch into the start position. A
thief may also use a dent puller (slide-hammer) to defeat
the locking mechanism. A dent puller is an auto body
repair tool used to pull out dents in the sheet metal of a
vehicle body. The tool is a 3-foot metal rod, approximately 1 1/2-inches in diameter, with a sliding weight that
moves the length of the rod. At one end of the tool is a
screw. The thief threads the screw into the key slot and

quickly draws the weight back from the ignition. The force created by this thrust rips the ignition lock right out of the steering column. He then inserts a screwdriver into the hole created by the removal of the ignition lock and turns it the same way a key is turned.

A second factor in the popularity of foreign cars is the speed of the vehicle (300 ZX, Mazda RX-7, Toyota Supra). Most auto thieves do not steal vehicles for simple joyrides. They steal them for a reason—either to strip them or to commit additional crimes such as drive-by shootings, armed robberies, or purse snatches. A fast car is desired for the getaway as well as for the salability of the parts.

Fads are a third factor. A particular car may be "in" with a certain crowd. A gang may have a rite of initiation requiring a wannabe to steal a certain model of car and then lure a police officer into a pursuit. The car may be used for a drive around a school dance or to impress women at a party.

Some older foreign vehicles have a problem with ignition wear which allows shaved-down or close-fitting keys to start the car. This usually applies to mid-seventies Datsun "Z" cars. The ignitions are so worn that anything close to the original key will start the vehicle.

American cars usually have stronger steering column locks, requiring a different approach. Often the column must be literally torn apart to access the ignition. The other method is to go up under the dash and "hot wire" the ignition wires.

Motorcycles are stolen the same way vehicles are. Pay close attention to ignitions while sitting at a stop light. Look for the telltale peeled or damaged ignition switch, with or without key. A rider who is unsteady on a bike or is obviously undersized for a particular model may signal the need for a closer look.

SMUGGLERS

In the southwestern states, the use of stolen vehicles for smuggling operations is popular. The vehicles used are commonly large American vans, pick-up trucks, Suburbans, and mini-vans. The vehicles are capable of off-road travel and are used for cross-border drug runs through the backcountry. They are often returned to Mexico for use in rural areas and on ranches. Vans with no side windows and mini-vans with tinted windows are commonly used to transport illegal aliens.

DRIVER PROFILE

The driver doesn't fit the car. A convict driving a new $20,000 car with college parking decals is a "profile" driver. The vehicle may not be stolen, but your job is not to rationalize the convict's ability to afford the car or to have student status. Your job is to inquire further into the status of the car.

Other driver profiles might include three gang members in a "Z" drive-by car or a long-haired, heavy-metal-type white male driving a pick-up truck with a country-western radio station bumper sticker.

Stereotypes exist because there is often a basis for them in reality. The reality of the world is that most convicts do not attend college. Gang members operate in groups and follow established patterns when engaging in criminal behavior (e.g., they steal similar cars as their cohorts). Most heavy-metal rockers listen to hard-rock stations, not country-western stations. Use local stereotypes to fashion your own profiles and then focus your attention on the vehicles and drivers that match.

VEHICLE DAMAGE

When a vehicle is stolen, it is often damaged or its appearance is altered for various reasons. Damage will usually occur during a forced entry into the vehicle and when it is started. The door and trunk locks may be pulled, as well as the ignition. A wing window, rear window, or back window may have been removed or broken out.

Experienced car thieves often prepare for the time

they must dump the car by initially removing from it anything of value. The first thing they do is strip it. The car stereo, the owner's personal prop-

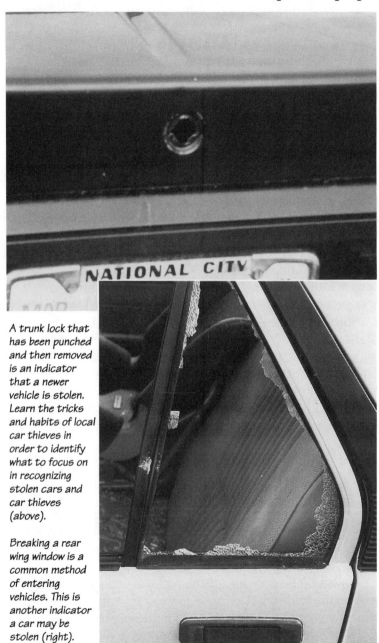

NATIONAL CITY

A trunk lock that has been punched and then removed is an indicator that a newer vehicle is stolen. Learn the tricks and habits of local car thieves in order to identify what to focus on in recognizing stolen cars and car thieves (above).

Breaking a rear wing window is a common method of entering vehicles. This is another indicator a car may be stolen (right).

erty, and expensive hubcaps are usually the first things to go. Then they remove the trunk lock and take car phones, sports equipment, and

removable stereos from the trunk. They even remove body parts, such as fenders and windows. They will then continue to drive the car, even after removing these parts, until they decide it is too "hot."

New vehicles tend to be well-maintained by their owners. They have worked hard for the money invested in the vehicle and pride themselves on a well-maintained appearance. Monthly car washes and wax jobs are routine for the first year. Unrepaired broken windows, broken locks, missing fenders, or other body parts are replaced quickly. Improperly maintained new vehicles indicate a closer look is necessary.

Street Tip: When looking over a profile vehicle, focus on the little things. Why does the new Chevy pick-up

This is an extreme case of a stripped vehicle that is still drivable. Profile vehicles with missing parts are indicators that a car may be stolen. Note that the rear passenger tire in this case is the spare. The regular tire was stolen and the spare used to keep the vehicle drivable.

need a portable radio on the dash for music? The majority of cars today have in-dash stereos, but maybe this has already had its radio stripped and the auto thief still wants to hear some music. Why is the trunk lock missing on a 1992 Nissan Maxima? The owner of such a new car doesn't pull the lock when he loses the trunk key; he calls a locksmith. How about the 300ZX with four missing hubcaps? The owner might lose one on a rough road, but not all four.

"THE CLUB"

A steering wheel locking mechanism like "the club" is an effective auto theft deterrence but is not foolproof. The common method for removing the club is to lie on the front seat and kick at it, forcing it off the steering wheel. The thief may also resort to using a dent puller on its lock or simply swinging this tool against it.

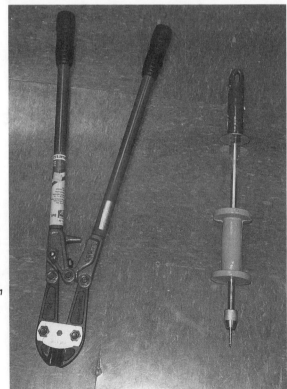

Dent puller used to remove ignition switch and bolt cutters for removing "the club" or cutting the steering wheel.

This type of force commonly results in a cracked window where the club is forced against it. Look for cracks on the driver's side, most

often lateral and a foot or more in length. Thieves have also been known to take a steering wheel off the steering column or cut it with bolt cutters to remove the locking device.

A commercially available device used to defeat all clubs is a master key called the "Anti-Club." Depending on your jurisdiction's statutes, this key may be considered a "burglary tool" and possession of one a criminal offense.

Car alarms are effective deterrents for the less-sophisticated car thief who is easily spooked. The professional, however, is aware of the nonchalant attitude most people have toward such alarms. The professional will simply raise the hood and remove wires connected to the horn

Ignition cut-off switches are simple, cheap, and effective.

or go under the dash and clip the offending wires.

Street Tip: Ignition cut-off switches appear to be the most effective theft-prevention devices. Once the car has been forcibly entered and the steering column lock defeated, the thief's "time on target" is up. When the vehicle fails to start, minimal time will be spent looking for the switch. Advise citizens of this low cost ($2 switch, 4' of wire) effective device.

AVOIDING DETECTION

Car thieves are well aware of the time gap between the car being reported stolen and the information being entered into the NCIC computer system. For the first day, thieves may be careless and not take any preventative measures to avoid detection. However, after the first day they often switch license plates with "cool" plates (those not yet reported stolen).

The sophisticated thief may steal license plates for the same make and model as the stolen car. If an officer runs both a stolen vehicle and registration check, then everything will appear normal. In a nonstop situation, an officer should anticipate such a move and compare the name of the registered owner with the race of the driver. A Vietnamese driver of a vehicle with a Hispanic registered owner should raise a flag.

A second flag is an older plate on a newer vehicle. Often an older vehicle will have newer license plates because it has been sold, reregistered, and issued new plates. However, the reverse is never true. Accustom yourself to matching the year of the vehicle with the type of plate. Be cognitive of the year license-plate styles changed. You may also see commercial plates on passenger vehicles and vice-versa.

UNREPORTED STOLEN VEHICLES

If you stop a suspected stolen vehicle and run a check on it but it does not come back as being reported stolen,

The use of a dummy key or key ring to cover ignition damage is common. Be sure to inspect the ignition, removing either of these. Red flags for such a trick include the inability of the driver to turn the engine off and the possession of only a single key .

Pay close attention to the ignition switch and steering column of vehicles you stop. Any damage to these areas may indicate the switch has been forced and the car is stolen. The entire keyhole of this ignition switch has been removed.

focus on the ignition and the license plates. At the appropriate time, closely examine the ignition and steering column. A common deceptive measure used to hide a punched ignition is to reinsert the pulled ignition switch and then insert a dummy key into it. The giveaways are damage to the column, the car cannot be shut off, and

Often the result of forcing an ignition switch is its easy removal from the steering column. The switch is now useless and may either be replaced to cover the damage or discarded. Look for the discarded switch when searching the stolen car. The fact that the switch is present is evidence of the driver's knowledge that the car was stolen (top right).

Changing ignition switches is a common technique used for stealing cars. The original switch is forced from the steering column and unplugged from its electrical connection. The thief then plugs in the switch he has brought with him. He has a key to his ignition switch (bottom right).

there's only one key. Most people carry their car keys on a key ring with multiple keys.

Check the license plate to see if it has been tampered with, the numbers have been altered, or it has been removed and switched recently. Oftentimes crooks are lazy and will only replace the rear plate. Look for a miss-

Comparison of the thief's ignition switch with key (top) and the original ignition switch after removal from the steering column. Search the recovered stolen car for the original switch to establish that the driver was aware the vehicle was stolen (top left).

Side view of a punched and then removed ignition switch (bottom left).

ing front plate or one that doesn't match the rear.

Ask the driver who the registered owner is and his address. Finally, if need be, send an officer by the registered owner's house to find out if it is indeed an unreported stolen vehicle.

THE STOP

Once you decide to stop the vehicle, ensure you have proper reasonable suspicion to do so if it is an unreported stolen vehicle. Primarily, the reasonable suspicion will consist of equipment, registration, or driving violations. Be particularly conscious of minor equipment violations, such as a license plate light that's out, a missing left-hand mirror, a missing gas cap, an obstruction hanging from rearview mirror, and so on.

If the vehicle is a reported auto theft, conduct a "hot stop." Forget the propaganda you have heard about auto theft being harmless or only a property crime. Car thieves steal for a reason—often violent crimes—and are just as dangerous as other felons. Always conduct a hot stop on a stolen car. A hot stop on an unreported stolen is advisable if the profile match is strong. Remember, a little dirt on an innocent person's knees is better than a dead cop.

While following a suspected stolen car, watch for suspicious behavior of occupants indicative of a stolen car. The passengers will remove their seat belts to expedite a getaway when the car stops, and they will turn their heads to watch you. The driver will begin to make evasive turns, and his eyes will be watching every move you make in the rearview mirror.

Once the police car is behind the suspect vehicle, the driver will almost immediately make the first right turn available. This movement is simple and is done to avoid police scrutiny. Make note of any turns made that do not fit the area or original direction of travel. A suspect who is driving in circles is obviously trying to avoid you.

Take your time making the stop. Call for additional units and start a helicopter and canine unit your way. Keep your microphone in your lap and talk down to it. As soon as the occupants see it at your mouth, the chase will be on. Auto thieves hope against all odds that you are not onto them, but as soon as they see you on the radio they know they will soon be surrounded by police cars.

If the car yields and is not reported as stolen, but you elect not to conduct a hot stop, follow this procedure to avoid being left behind on a "sucker stop": exit your vehicle quickly, as you have been trained to do, but remain at the driver's door. Watch and listen to determine whether the suspect's car is running. Check to see if

This vehicle's brake lights are on, indicating the car is probably still in gear and ready to roll. Stay at your driver's door and order the driver to turn off the engine.

the brake lights are on and whether the car is a stick or automatic. If it's a stick and the brake lights are on, the car is probably in gear and ready to roll. If it's an automatic, watch for the white back-up lights to come on—it means the driver has put the car in park. Stay at your car and command the driver to turn the ignition off and remove the key. Often car thieves will yield to sucker the cop out of his car and get the jump in the pursuit. Be prepared for this maneuver.

THE PURSUIT

This will not be an in-depth discussion on pursuit patterns. The initial goal of the auto thief is to shake the police then dump the car as fast as possible. The thief knows once he's free of the vehicle, association with a stolen car is difficult. The rare thief is one who continues to drive the car after evading the police.

Pursuits most commonly end in a crash. Let the crook be the one to crash first. These drivers are often less skilled at high-speed driving than police officers. Maintain your cool and don't drive over your head.

Keep a safe distance between you and the car—25 yards or more. This distance will allow you to maneuver around an accident or prepare for evasive maneuvers, such as quick, unanticipated turns.

A safe distance also reduces the risk of injury to civilians. The closer your car is, the more pressured the suspect will feel. Running red lights or stop signs without any slowing will be the result. This banzai-type driving is avoidable if pressure on the driver is reduced.

The most common mistake a suspect driver will make in a high-speed chase is taking corners too tight and fast. As he comes out of the turn, his vehicle cannot maintain the curve and slides out of control. Avoid this problem by taking turns slow and wide. Accelerate midturn to maintain traction and get a burst of speed. Watch for other cop cars behind you trying to take the lead when you swing wide.

The suspect will most often make right turns during the chase. This averts the need to cross traffic and places a visual barrier between him and the police. Keep this in mind when anticipating a turn or if you have lost the suspect.

At night, once the thief has put some distance between the stolen car and the police, he will "blackout," or shut

Slow down!

off the lights. Focus attention on the
red glare of brake lights and their
reflection off windows, parked cars,
and reflective street signs as the sus-

pect makes several turns to lose you. If you lose the suspect, stop and turn off your engine. Listen for the sound
of the car and direction of travel.

Once the vehicle has stopped, focus on the suspect
driver bailing out of the car. Quickly make note of his
physical appearance and clothing. This fleeting glimpse
will be critical in later identifying who the driver was.
Remember, the district attorney normally will only file
auto theft charges against the driver, not the passengers.

You and your partner should pursue the driver
together for safety reasons. Direct your partner to broadcast the suspect's description and direction of travel
while you are both running. Your responsibility will be
to keep the suspect in sight. The second police vehicle
in a pursuit, usually the one responsible for calling the
pursuit, should immediately direct officers in setting
up a perimeter.

Critical in capturing a fleeing suspect is prior coordi-
nation with fellow officers. Discuss at lineup what the
role of each officer should be during a vehicle pursuit
and subsequent inevitable foot chase. Once the pursuit is
underway and the initial excitement has worn off, then
coordinate briefly with a minimum of air time what each
officer's role will be:

"114Y, we have the driver," "115X, we'll take the passenger," "116Y, we'll set up the perimeter and dispatch;
start a canine unit this way."

THE REPORT

Once the suspect is in custody and the officer has
cooled down, focus on establishing the suspect's knowledge that the car was stolen. This is the key element in a
stolen vehicle charge. Make detailed notes and photograph evidence of punched ignitions, broken windows,
stripped parts, no keys, etc. Look for gang graffiti written
in the car, often on the sun visors.

Separate and interrogate the driver and passengers with the same goal in mind. Obtain a statement as to that night's events and ownership of the vehicle. Inconsistent statements may indicate guilty knowledge you need as well as assist in obtaining a confession.

ADDENDUM TO AUTO THEFT ARREST REPORT

Continued from ARR/JUV. CON.

				PAGE	of	CASE NUMBER

CODE SECTION	MONTH	DAY	YEAR	DAY OF WEEK	TIME

VICTIM	SUSPECT	PROPERTY TAG NO.

OFFICER'S INVESTIGATION

I asked the following questions of the suspect, passengers and witnesses and carefully noted the responses on my Arrest Report. At the point that I determined the vehicle might be stolen or that I knew I would arrest the subject for any offense, I admonished him of his rights.

☐ Yes ☐ No 1. May I see your driver's license?

☐ Yes ☐ No 2. Is this your vehicle?

☐ Yes ☐ No 3. May I see the vehicle registration?

☐ Yes ☐ No 4. Where did you get the vehicle?

☐ Yes ☐ No 5. When did you get the vehicle?

☐ Yes ☐ No 6. Whose vehicle is it?

☐ Yes ☐ No 7. Why do you have the vehicle?

☐ Yes ☐ No 8. Where does the registered owner live?

☐ Yes ☐ No 9. When were you going to take the vehicle back?

☐ Yes ☐ No 10. How were you going to return the vehicle?

☐ Yes ☐ No 11. Where is the ignition key?

☐ Yes ☐ No 12. How did you get it started?

☐ Yes ☐ No 13. Who is the "John Doe" who gave you the vehicle?

☐ Yes ☐ No 14. Who else was present and saw you get the vehicle from "John Doe"?

☐ Yes ☐ No 15. Who else knows "John Doe"?

Key to making an auto theft case against a suspect is establishing the fact that the suspect knew the car was stolen. The questions and procedures on this form are designed to establish such knowledge.

A vehicle pursuit is not worth your life or that of a innocent civilian. There is a distinct possibility that you will strike a child, other pedestrians, or another vehicle when you drive at high speed, no matter how careful you are. There just isn't enough time to react. Adrenaline and the thrill of the chase cloud your judgment.

Never allow yourself to become so fixated on the capture as to overcome common sense. Drive with the thought in mind, "If this becomes too dangerous I'll drop

---

Addendum to Auto Theft Report
Page Two

If you checked no on any of the above questions, please explain:

_____
_____
_____

I additionally did the following as part of my investigation:

☐ Yes ☐ No 1. Examined the ignition switch.

☐ Yes ☐ No 2. Examined the vehicle for damaged locks, window breakage and missing accessories.

☐ Yes ☐ No 3. Admonished the suspect.

☐ Yes ☐ No 4. Is an interpreter required (make every attempt to find one.)

☐ Yes ☐ No 5. Reports from other officers submitted? (Includes supervisors.)

☐ Yes ☐ No 6. Does suspect have knowledge that vehicle is stolen?

☐ Yes ☐ No 7. Did you investigate the stolen plates?

☐ Yes ☐ No 8. Who saw the suspect driving?

☐ Yes ☐ No 9. Did you get officers full names, ID numbers?

☐ Yes ☐ No 10. Did the victim give anyone permission to drive or have the vehicle?

Additional comments:

_____
_____
_____

REPORTING OFFICER	I.D. #	DIVISION
DATE OF REPORT Month · Day / Year TIME	APPROVED BY:	

the pursuit." Run that thought through your mind after the initial adrenaline dump occurs. Then relax, breathe slowly and deeply, talk to yourself, and maintain a safe distance from the suspect car.

SUMMARY

1. Establish a stolen vehicle and auto thief profile based on local training and experience.

2. Look for vehicle damage associated with auto theft, including punched trunk, door, and ignition locks.

3. Ignition cut-off switches are the most effective theft deterrents.

4. On unreported stolen vehicles, closely examine ignition switches and license plates.

5. Hot stops should be conducted on all stolen cars.

6. Wait for cover, helicopters, and dogs before initiating a stolen vehicle stop.

7. Wait for the suspect's car engine to be shut off before approaching the stolen vehicle.

8. Keep your distance during a pursuit.

9. Foot pursuits of the driver should be conducted by both officers.

10. Coordinate with other officers before the foot chase.

11. Once the suspect is in custody, focus on getting statements and evidence indicating the suspect knew the car was stolen.

12. Photograph a punched-out ignition.

13. Don't hesitate to discontinue an ultrahazardous pursuit.

CHAPTER 6 PATROL OFFICER INVESTIGATIONS

t's start of shift, and you decide to check up on a few of your "regulars." While you're at the station, you run them for warrants and search-and-seizure waivers. You find one of your favorites, James Hendrix, has been arrested for car burglary recently. This piques your curiosity, because he would need a method to fence any of the stolen property. You run a pawn check on him. This computer search will reveal any items he has recently sold to pawnshops or second-hand stores in the area.

A thief needs a method of converting stolen property into cash. The most common sources for this cash are "street" sales, swap meets, professional fences, or pawnshops. Pawnshops are often overlooked by police officers as a depository for stolen goods because of their legitimacy. However, some shop owners frequently turn a blind

Pawnshops are a source of information as well as a repository for stolen property. Focus citizen contacts and patrol activity around them.

eye to obviously stolen goods or are outright crooks themselves.

Among the controls placed on pawnshops are the requirements that a pawn slip be filled out on every item bought or pawned and that identification be provided when an item is pawned. The pawn slip is then sent to the police department, where the information is entered into the computer under the subject's name.

Checks are run on items with serial numbers to see if they have been reported stolen. There are two problems with this system. One is that the item's owner, the reporting officer, the data entry personnel, and the shopkeeper must record the serial number correctly and in a timely manner. Any error along the way will void the check. The second problem is that many items do not have serial numbers or the numbers were never recorded. Without the serial number, searching for an item reported stolen is like looking for a Ford at the Super Bowl.

However, checking stolen reports of unique items may circumvent this problem. Under those circumstances, few items will come up in your search. With this narrow field of possibilities, the owners may be contacted and asked to identify the piece of property in person.

In the case of Mr. Hendrix, you find he has recently sold a guitar to a music shop. Now the most you know about a guitar is that it is a musical instrument with strings. However, you do *know* Mr. Hendrix is *not* a guitar player.

The next step is to determine whether Mr. Hendrix's guitar has been reported stolen. Overall you're good with the computers, but in the area of property searches you are weak. To run a successful search for stolen property, you need to know the proper computer nomenclature for it. For this knowledge you go to your friends in Crime Analysis. They punch in the information from the pawn slip, and a car burglary report with the same type of guitar comes up.

You're pleased with the results, but Mr. Hendrix isn't knitting sweaters in the local lockup yet. You call the victim and ask for identifying marks on the guitar, such as scratches, decals, engravings, etc. You then arrange to meet at the music store so he can identify the guitar in person.

This is the touchy part. If the guitar is his, then it goes to him and the shop owner is out his "buy" money. To ensure no arguments take place in the shop, you tell the victim not to comment about the identification in front of the shop owner.

You walk inside and have the guitar brought down off a shelf. The guitar matches the description given by the victim over the phone. You photograph it with the victim and release it to him. The shop owner isn't happy, but then he probably should never have paid $35 for a $500 guitar.

You now have two avenues by which to resolve this case. The simplest is to take to the streets to arrest Hendrix for possession of stolen property. The identification of the guitar as stolen property, combined with the identification provided during the "sale," provides the probable cause necessary for a street arrest.

You keep in mind that an arrest warrant is required to arrest him in his home if you go there with probable cause and the intent to arrest. An exception is if you go to the residence under exigent circumstances or without probable cause and develop it once you're there.

The second method is to contact Mr. Hendrix, either at home or on the street, and obtain a handwriting exemplar. The results of a successful comparison will provide additional evidence of his guilt and pave the way for obtaining an arrest warrant.

You decide to contact him at his residence and obtain a handwriting exemplar. You direct him to write his name as written on the original pawn slip (this slip may also contain his thumbprint, as required in some jurisdictions). The handwriting expert must have signatures from the suspect which compare letter for letter to the one on the pawn slip. He can't compare apples and oranges. Simply allowing the suspect to write what he purports to be his signature will give him the leeway to use abbreviations, initials, scribblings, etc. The suspect knows what you want but will feign cooperation in an attempt to dispel suspicion about him. He will use any method he can to subvert your investigation without being obvious about it. You must therefore be very controlling in handling the process.

You don't show him the slip. This prevents him from providing a dissimilar sample signature. This tack also prevents him from later claiming that he simply copied the signature as directed, so that is why they matched.

You have him sign his name 40 times. The reason for this is that you are looking for his true signature. Initially, he may attempt to alter it, but the more he writes the lazier he gets. The later sample signatures should then be closer to his true signature. Both the original pawn slip and the samples are submitted to a handwriting expert. The expert concludes both were written by the same person, Mr. Hendrix.

Before going through the time-consuming process of submitting a request for an arrest warrant, you take to the streets looking for Mr. Hendrix. You pick him up at the local open-air drugstore within an hour.

THE NEED AND OPPORTUNITY

Because of unmanageable caseloads, time delays, laziness, and ineptness, crime cases often are not investigated adequately. Recall senior officers saying, "Ah, just drop a note to the dicks (detectives); they'll do the follow-up." *Wrong.* Any honest detective, detective supervisor, or police manager will admit that solvable crimes are left to die in some desk drawer.

What you can do about it is become your own investigator. You have radio calls to respond to, but as we all know, even in the busiest divisions there is often a lot of dead time. Plan to conduct your own follow-ups during this time. Day watch is particularly suitable for such work because of the low number of calls that come in before noon. Victims and witnesses are awake, and businesses are open.

Delay in investigating a crime is often the deciding factor in whether the case will ever be solved. As little as a few hours may determine whether the suspect is ever arrested. Memories fade, evidence is destroyed, stolen property disposed of, alibis formulated, vehicles sold, and so on. This short time window puts the patrol officer in the best position to solve the crime.

Another curious facet of quick apprehension of criminals is that it increases the likelihood that they will confess. It seems that the closer in time to their commission of the crime, the greater their need or desire to confess. As time elapses, their sense of guilt or other impetus to confess decreases, so timely capture and interrogation are essential in securing adequate evidence to convict.

WHERE TO START

Investigating a crime case is as simple as placing yourself in the position of the detective who will eventually be assigned the case. Detectives have no magical abilities or talents. They simply follow up on the leads generated by your initial investigation. There is little to prevent you from doing the same thing.

You have access to phones, the same computers, and the same investigative support units as the detective does. You simply need to learn what is available and from whom. When you take a burglary report and there are no fingerprints and no witnesses, the crime is not likely to be solved by you or a detective.

However, if you investigate a drive-by shooting and the shooter has been identified as "Chuey" from the "Eastside" gang, then you have a lead you can follow up on. Three sources for you to contact are your gang unit, the computer's nickname file, and an east-side beat officer. Any of these sources may tell you who "Chuey" is. A stakeout of his residence is then in order. Each of these courses of action is readily available to a patrol officer.

Street Tip: Learning to investigate a crime begins with learning to think like a criminal as well as a detective. Learning to think like a criminal is as simple as planning your own burglary or robbery. Case a 7-11 on your beat as if you were going to rob it. Ask yourself: where would I park? In which direction would I flee? Who could be a witness, either knowingly or unknowingly? How long would I need to be inside?

Answers to these questions dictate from which direction you'll approach the scene, what path you'll trace as you walk the suspect's avenue of escape, and whom you will question. These efforts may provide you with possible stakeout locations for arriving officers, discarded disguises, or other evidence and witnesses who saw the getaway car but didn't connect it with a robbery.

Training officers should employ this technique with their trainees. Have the trainee "burglarize" a cooperative person's residence. Ask the trainee how he would get in, where he would touch and leave fingerprints, which way he would flee, whether he would "stash" some of the loot for later recovery, etc.

SUSPECT ADDRESSES

Often with follow-ups, a suspect may be identified, but a residence may be difficult to locate. Driver's license and vehicle registration records are a great

source for most such information.
But this information is often out-of-
date due to the transiency of criminals. However, the old address can
provide a starting point for your investigation.

Contact the mother or father, the apartment manager, or the current occupant. Find out if the suspect left a forwarding address. Talk with neighbors to find out if they have a forwarding address. Run their names and license plate numbers through your computer's field interview files. These files often provide the most updated addresses on criminals. Contact a subject's parole officer. Parole officers frequently conduct home interviews with parolees and have accurate addresses for them. Other sources easily available through a phone call are postal inspectors, the gas company, and the water company.

As far as your responsibilities as a patrol officer go with regard to radio calls, the apprehension of a felony suspect should take priority over most anything else. Most supervisors will be reluctant to call off an aggressive investigation of a fresh felony. Put in two hours sitting on the suspect's house. Such work may not pay off all the time, but it will often be enough to make up for the times you miss locking up the crook.

Street Tip: Girlfriends' residences are popular hideouts for criminals after a recent crime. They feel safer there, operating under the belief that the police will be focusing on their residences rather than those of their girlfriends. During computer checks, look for female companions' names and run address checks on them. Questioning of witnesses should at some point concentrate on the suspect's known girlfriends.

LICENSE PLATES

Partial and full license plate numbers are the most common type of suspect information that lends itself to patrol follow-up. Here are two examples.

An officer was working patrol, and an all-units broadcast went over the air regarding an assault with a deadly weapon. The broadcast described the car involved and its license plate number. The plate came back to a car dealership. However, the report unit was not interested in following the lead. "Leave it to the detectives," he said.

"Give me a break," the officer thought. He drove to the dealership and contacted the sales manager. The sales manager told him the car had been sold recently and gave him the buyer's address. The officer drove the 3 miles to the residence, and the car was parked in front. (At this point the officer doesn't have probable cause to arrest the owner, so there is no need for an arrest warrant or any way to obtain one. Ramey (see Chapter 1) does not apply because of this, so the officer can still contact the owner in his residence. If the officer develops probable cause at that point, he can then arrest the owner out of his home.)

The officer made the contact, the owner confessed, and the weapon was recovered. A day or two later, the suspect would have disposed of the weapon and established his alibi. The reporting officer was amazed the arrest was made, but there was nothing amazing about it, just a little extra work.

A second illustration of patrol detective work is another assault-with-a-deadly-weapon case. A male was stabbed at a Jack-in-the-Box by another male and an Hispanic female. The witnesses were interviewed at the hospital. They gave a license plate number but weren't sure of one of the digits. One witness described the car as a gray Ford Galaxy; the other said it was a gray Plymouth Valiant.

Both witnesses were sure of their descriptions, but the second stated he knew it was a Valiant because he had owned one previously. (Anyone who has owned a particular type of automobile before can tell it apart from the crowd just like a mother sheep can spot her lamb in a flock of a hundred.) The officer went with the Valiant. He ran the partial plate eliminating the questionable digit. He had 10 possibles. One was for a Plymouth. The driver, who had recently received a traffic ticket in the car, had been an Hispanic female. The officer drove by the house, and she was just getting back into the car. The weapon was on the front seat.

Often crime victims will state that they have seen the suspect in the neighborhood before or that the person hangs out at a certain street corner or liquor store. Whether the case is fresh or stale, take half an hour and drive the victim around the neighborhood. There's a chance you may come across the subject, and, at the very least, you have shown the victim you care. This may be enough to alleviate the mental anguish he has suffered.

At the minimum, give victims/witnesses a phone number where you can be contacted—preferably a pager number. Knowing they have immediate access to someone familiar with the incident and in a position to help them makes them more inclined to take a more active role in the investigation. They'll make extra trips to the rec center or the liquor store to look for the suspect. They'll talk to more of their friends and neighbors about the suspect and may identify him on their own. Showing you care will make it easier for them to care.

CLASS RINGS

One of the highest targeted items in residential burglaries is jewelry. Gold jewelry is particularly desirable because of the ease with which it can be pawned or sold. Stolen gold jewelry is often sold for its weight to coin shops and pawn shops. The shop holds the jewelry for

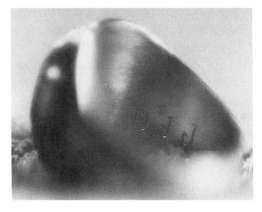

The initials engraved on the band of a class ring can be the key to identifying its owner. A phone call to the school and a check of the graduating class of the year inscribed on the ring will give you the name of the owner.

30 days in order to allow a police check to be run on it. Then they melt it down and sell it.

Since most jewelry is fairly generic, it is rarely identified as being stolen. Class rings are one exception. These rings have the name of the school, the year of graduation, and the owner's initials engraved on the band. Identifying the true owner requires a phone call to the school.

Schools maintain yearbook libraries. Ask a school employee to thumb through the appropriate yearbook looking for a graduate with those initials. Once the owner is identified, verify by phone or in person that the ring has been stolen.

Often police officers will run across some very nefarious individuals wearing class rings. Pay close attention to them. If the guy is wearing a female class ring on his small finger, a closer inspection is in order. This inspection may be considered a search. Be sure to obtain consent or probable cause to examine the ring, then look for the identifiers.

POSSESSION OF STOLEN PROPERTY

Police officers frequently enter the residences of citizens in response to radio calls, follow-up inquiries, and disturbances. During such visits, keep an eye out for contraband left in plain sight. As with a pimp wearing a U.S. Naval Academy class ring, a $2,000 stereo system in a unemployed laborer's studio apartment should raise a red flag. If a piece of property doesn't "fit the picture," follow your instincts. Take a closer look at it. Look for an engraved driver's license number, Social Security number, or serial number. Remember, moving the item or clearing away obstacles may be considered a search; you will need consent or a search warrant.

The charge of possession of stolen property hinges on the suspect *knowingly* possessing stolen property. The key to making this charge stick is obtaining statements indicating such knowledge. It is unlikely that the suspect will admit to knowing the property is stolen. The suspect will probably lie. However, those lies may be inconsistent with the facts of the case that point toward this knowledge.

For example, ask the suspect when the property was acquired. Do so in a manner that makes suspects think they will be exonerated but that will actually make the case. If you know the item was stolen only recently, ask, "So, you've had this ring since you graduated 5 years ago?" or "So, your friend gave this ring to you a couple of months ago?" Since an affirmative response is inconsistent with the established fact of the recent theft, it can be inferred that the suspect was aware the property was stolen—*the* critical element in a possession-of-stolen-property case.

VICTIM IDENTIFICATION

Criminals have an unusual habit of keeping the victim's identification after a theft. In most purse and wallet thefts, the thief empties the pocketbook of the money and the ID and then discards the pocketbook immediately. The identification probably assists the thief in passing forged checks or using the stolen credit cards. However, once he discards the checks and credit cards, he leaves the remaining identification lying around.

Frequently an officer will run across a victim's gym membership card or library card on the floorboard of a suspect's car. These may be the keys to a solvable crime. If the victim has reported the theft, it's a simple matter to run a check on the victim's name to determine the type and nature of the crime.

The problem usually arises when the victim has failed to report the theft or is unaware of it. An officer should then use the same resources to identify a victim as he would to locate a criminal. A phone call to the gym may provide a home or business phone number. If the person you contact is unwilling to give out the info over the phone, then either drive there to get it in person or leave your number. Then have the clerk call the victim.

Even if a case cannot be made against the suspect, you will be able to return the items to a grateful victim.

Scan a street thug's residence and vehicle for identification. Oftentimes it belongs to a previous victim.

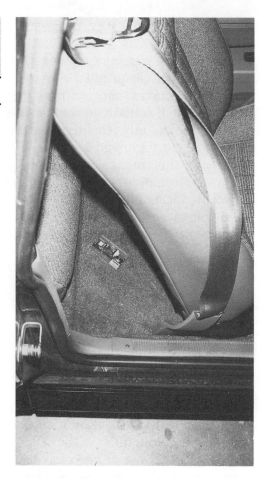

EASY FELONIES

Two felonies patrol officers often overlook are possession of a handgun by an ex-felon and petty theft with a prior theft conviction. In some states, illegal possession of a handgun is a misdemeanor, and shoplifting is also a misdemeanor. The result of such arrests may be a field release on a citation or a low-bail booking into county jail. The felony charges can be added if the patrol officer can document the prior convictions.

Shoplifting is often a crime of teenagers and professional thieves. The first category is easily distinguishable from the latter. This latter group is mostly made up of junkies. They often operate in pairs, with one as the lookout and the other concealing merchandise in a package or on his person. The property may be sold on the street or brought to the return desk of the victim's store.

Property taken includes cigarettes, liquor, and trendy clothing—items that will sell quickly on the street.

SAN DIEGO POLICE DEPARTMENT

CONTINUED FROM
☐ ARR./JUV. CON.
☐ CRIME
☐ OFFICER'S REPORT
☐ _____

Theft/Shoplift Addendum Report

PAGE ___ OF ___   CASE NUMBER ___

CODE SECTION AND DESCRIPTION   MONTH | DAY | YEAR | DAY OF WEEK | TIME

LOCATION OF INCIDENT   CITY   ZIP   BEAT

PERSONS INVOLVED: VICTIM   SUSPECT   PROPERTY TAG #'S

ORIGIN/OFFICERS STATEMENT: ON THIS DATE I RESPONDED TO _____ TO TAKE
(STORE NAME AND LOCATION)

CUSTODY OF A THEFT SUSPECT THAT _____ HAD TAKEN INTO CUSTODY FOR:
(SECURITY OFFICER/CITIZEN)

SHOPLIFT ☐ BURGLARY ☐ UPON MY ARRIVAL, I SPOKE WITH _____, WHO TOLD ME THE FOLLOWING:

(BRIEF SYNOPSIS. ONLY) _____

_____

_____

_____

_____

SEE THE ATTACHED WRITTEN STATEMENT BY _____ FOR SPECIFIC INFORMATION
(SECURITY OFFICER/CITIZEN)

CONCERNING THE CITIZEN'S ARREST.

A RECORDS CHECK WAS ☐ WAS NOT ☐ CONDUCTED BY OFFICER: _____ (IF NO
(OFFICER'S NAME ONLY)

RECORDS CHECK WAS CONDUCTED, WHY NOT?) _____

IT WAS DETERMINED THAT THE SUSPECT HAD ☐ HAD NOT ☐ SERVED TIME FOR A THEFT RELATED OFFENSE PER SECTION 666 P.C.).

DISPOSITION: I TOOK CUSTODY OF _____, WHO WAS
☐ ISSUED MISDEMEANOR CITATION # _____, AND RELEASED ON HIS WRITTEN PROMISE TO APPEAR.
☐ BOOKED INTO COUNTY JAIL. (BOOKING # _____).
☐ BOOKED INTO LAS COLINAS WOMEN'S DETENTION FACILITY. (BOOKING # _____).
☐ TAKEN TO JUVENILE HALL. ☐ OTHER _____ .

VICTIM/WITNESS STATEMENTS: (SEE ATTACHED ARJIS-9 BY _____).

EVIDENCE: ☐ RETAINED BY _____
☐ IMPOUNDED AT _____ ON TAG # _____
OTHER _____

SUSPECT ADMONISHED?
☐ ANSWER QUESTION #1 _____
        QUESTION #2 _____
☐ NO. WHY NOT? _____

SUSPECT'S STATEMENT: (SEE REVERSE SIDE)

REPORTING OFFICER   I.D. # | DIVISION | APP. BY   MONTH | DAY | YEAR | TIME

CONT ☐

Critical in turning a simple misdemeanor shoplifting arrest into an easy felony is establishing that the suspect has a prior theft conviction with at least one day of time served.

A shoplifter in his or her late twenties or older is generally a professional. Your first concern will be to identify the suspect properly (Chapter 3). Your second concern will be to identify any prior theft convictions that resulted in his serving at least one day in jail. It may have been a felony or misdemeanor. If one is found, the subject may then be charged with the felony of petty theft with a prior.

If it is a local conviction, a notation in the report as to the case number and charge will put the assigned detective and deputy district attorney on notice. However, if the case is not local, you will have to conduct some follow-up work. To find out about nonlocal convictions, query the subject's state and FBI rap (criminal history) sheet. The FBI sheet maintains fairly accurate files as to disposition on criminal cases. This disposition is key to determining whether the suspect has served the necessary one day.

If you locate such a case, call the court clerk for the county in which the suspect was arrested. Ask for a certified copy of the case and its disposition showing the time served. Have it sent to the detective or deputy DA assigned to the case immediately. Any time lapse between booking and the receipt of the file gives the DA and the defense attorney an opportunity to avoid the felony charge.

The same procedure should be followed with an ex-felon in possession of a handgun or other applicable firearm.

Additional sources to be checked are state parole, federal parole, and BATF (Bureau of Alcohol, Tobacco and Firearms). BATF is aggressive in pursuing federal firearms violations against career criminals. Your misdemeanor possession of a concealed weapon firearms case may wind up being dropped at the state level and turned over to the feds for some serious time.

Keep in mind ex-felon statutes are very specific as to which charges constitute a proper "ex-felony." In reviewing an out-of-state rap sheet, be conscious of the differences in each state's definition of a particular crime. Call a local law-enforcement agency to verify the type of offense to be sure it coincides with your state statute.

93
PATROL OFFICER
INVESTIGATIONS

Establishing a liaison with federal enforcement agencies allows access to strong and unique criminal prosecution statutes as well as source funds for special projects.

DEPARTMENT OF THE TREASURY
BUREAU OF ALCOHOL, TOBACCO, AND FIREARMS

PROJECT ACHILLES

The Facts...

The Bureau of Alcohol, Tobacco and Firearms (ATF) enforces the Federal firearms laws pertaining to Armed Gang Members, Armed Career Criminals and Armed Narcotics Traffickers...

Violators are subject to enhanced mandatory sentences with <u>no</u> probation and <u>no</u> parole...

Offenders who possess three or more prior convictions for violent or potentially violent felonies, who are subsequently convicted of possessing a firearm, are subjected to a <u>mandatory prison term of 15 years to life.</u>

If the current incident of firearms possession is of a violent or potentially violent character, <u>the minimum sentence doubles to 30 years to life.</u>

A person who is convicted of using or carrying a firearm while trafficking in narcotics or while committing a violent felony is subjected to an <u>enhancement of from 5 years to life</u> consecutive to whatever is awarded for the underlying offense.

Through <u>PROJECT ACHILLES</u> ATF works hand-in-hand with State and local Law Enforcement agencies to suppress armed gang activity, armed narcotics trafficking and the armed career criminals by assisting these agencies in taking these cases through the Federal court system to obtain the enhanced "minimum-mandatory" sentences.

COMMONLY USED FEDERAL FIREARMS LAWS

VIOLATION	DESCRIPTION	PENALTY
18 USC 922(A)(6)	False statement by a prohibited person to acquire a firearm.	10 Years
18 USC 922(g)(1)	Convicted felon in possession of a firearm or ammunition.	10 Years
18 USC 922(g)(2)	Fugitive in possession of a firearm or ammunition.	10 Years
18 USC 922(g)(3)	Addict or drug user in possession of a firearm or ammunition.	10 Years
18 USC 922(g)(4)	Adjudicated mental defective in possession of a firearm.	10 Years
18 USC 924 (c)	Uses or carries firearm in crime of violence or drug trafficking.	Mandatory 5 years in addition to the substantive offense
	Uses or carries machine gun or silencer in such a crime	Mandatory 30 years
18 USC 924 (e)	Possession of a firearm by a person who has three or more convictions for violent or potentially violent felonies.	Mandatory 15 years to life
	If possessed by such a person while committing a violent or potentially violent act.	Mandatory 30 years to life
26 USC 5861 (d)	Possession of an unregistered machine gun, silencer, "bomb", "zip gun", short barrelled rifle or short barrelled shotgun.	10 Years

If you encounter these firearms violations or other questionable circumstances, and wish to discuss Federal prosecution, please contact...

Jim Allison

~~DOUG LAMBERT~~
SPECIAL AGENT

U.S. TREASURY DEPARTMENT
BUREAU OF ALCOHOL, TOBACCO & FIREARMS

880 FRONT ST., RM 4-N-10
SAN DIEGO, CA 92188

TEL: (619) 557-5608
FTS: 895-5608

A curious aspect of patrol officers conducting their own investigations is the negative attitude of the most overworked and the laziest of detectives. Once detectives are assigned a case, for some reason they become very territorial over *your* case. Play the game smart—throw them a bone and keep them apprised of the status of the case. They may have information or knowledge that will prevent duplication of effort or assist in locking the criminal up.

Investigations and follow-ups by patrol officers may not be required and are often subtly discouraged. You may not get a pat on the back, but it's the "right thing to do" and is one of the distinctions between an average cop and a good street cop.

SUMMARY

1. Conduct your own investigations to a logical conclusion.

2. Plan your own crimes so you can begin to think like a criminal.

3. Use nicknames, license plate numbers, and unique physical descriptions as starting points.

4. Once the suspect's identity is known, work to locate his residence or that of his girlfriend.

5. Stake out these locations for a minimum of two hours.

6. Enlist the assistance of victims and witnesses in the investigation. Give them directions on what to look for, such as direction of travel, clothing description, license plate number, etc.

7. Actively look for stolen property when dealing with hard-core criminals.

8. Run complete criminal history checks of suspects; they often lead to additional charges.

9. Carry a beeper so victims, witnesses, and informants can contact you immediately.

10. Use the same methods to identify a victim as you would for a suspect.

CHAPTER 7

NARCOTICS AND
THE STREET COP

en o'clock and you're on morning
junkie patrol. You're uniformed
patrol, and narcotics is your game.
This part of town doesn't have a
reputation of being a heroin-addict
haven, but kick a few rocks or shake some trees and
you'll find them.

You drive to addict central at Fairmont Avenue and
Myrtle. You slow to cruising speed and watch for the
profile. Male in his late twenties, early thirties; talking
slowly to no one; no lunch box or briefcase in his hands;
long-sleeve shirt; and the tan but emotionless face of
someone who's spent time catching rays in Soledad's
exercise yard. You've developed this profile from
literally hundreds of arrests of heroin addicts.

Heroin is the drug of the older set. Most users don't
start until their early twenties, which is old by drug-
abuser standards. Forget what you've seen on "Geraldo";

teenagers just don't shoot "chiva." They start around 19 or 20, and their habit builds more quickly than their income. By 23, 24, they're spending their first set of 18, 24, or 36 months in prison. When they get out, they have the "look" of a hard-core criminal. They're "buffed," their hair is cut short, and their "tracked-up" arms are tattooed.

It takes about 15 minutes to find your first possible target. He's walking southbound on Fairmont while you drive by going north. You watch his face closely, and he doesn't change his expression. He's looking right through you. Bingo, now you have target lock-on.

The average citizen watches the police like a gazelle watches a lion. The gazelle knows the lion is not going to attack, and the gazelle is not worried. But he is curious as to whom the next victim will be. A convict/junkie is more like the nervous ostrich—bury the head (i.e., don't make eye contact) and hope the cop keeps going.

You note junkie Rick is moving slowly, not the brisk walk of someone going to work. He has that "just woke up" look about him. You turn around and drive right up behind him. He's wearing a button-down shirt with three-quarter-length sleeves. You know exactly what you're looking for. From 10 feet away you see "tracks" and the tail end of peacock feathers tattooed on his forearm—a prison tattoo just visible at the sleeve's edge.

This isn't exactly overpowering evidence of Rick's guilt for being under the influence of heroin, but it will justify a "stop." You stop and talk to Rick, and he is pleasant. Junkies, for the most part, are relatively pleasant to deal with. They know the rules of the game and are cooperative. This is due to the calming effect of heroin and the sophistication they have acquired from time in prison.

Rick readily identifies himself and agrees to allow you to examine his arms. He has several 3- to 4-inch lines of scar tissue (tracks) over veins on his left forearm. The peacock was an attempt to conceal these marks.

Scarring over the veins of IV drug users leaves what is called "silver streaking." The tattoo of this woman was probably in place before the streaking occurred, as the streak has little tattoo ink left. The repeated injections destroyed that small portion of the tattoo.

You're looking for the "fresh" needle marks from his "wake-up" injection. There are several red marks on his biceps in various stages of scabbing, indicating they are too old to have been responsible for putting him "under the influence." You're looking for the mark three to four hours old, one that may be weeping a clear liquid or even bleeding. You have no luck finding one.

You notice his speech is slow but also slurred. Slow speech is indicative of heroin, but slurred is not. You pick up a whiff of alcohol on his breath. His morning pick-me-up is looking more like a six-pack than a "quarter" of heroin.

Your last shot is the eyes—more accurately, his pupils. Small pupils (2mm-2.9mm) you win; larger than that, he wins. One problem: it's daylight, and an accurate pupil test isn't possible. You need controlled lighting conditions.

This is where Mr. Congeniality's cooperation comes

into play. You explain the problem
with the eye test and ask if he will
ride to the station with you. "No
problem," he says.

You know this guy is a bad guy. He is not sure if you
know it. But he does know once you do find out, the gig
is up. He will polish your badge to keep you from
finding out.

So far you have accepted his word for who he is; he
has no identification. Since he is being so cooperative,
you ask if you can stop by his residence to pick up his
identification. Once again, "No problem." He says he is
staying with his sister, and you drive the short distance
to her house. You escort him to his room.

He points out a dresser drawer as containing his
identification. You rummage through it and don't find
the ID. However, you do find a checkbook with another
person's name on it. Rick volunteers he found it. Right.

This is looking better all the time. The reason you go
after junkies is that their whole lives consist of one
crime after another. From the minute they wake to when
they fall asleep, they are stealing, shooting dope, or
selling dope. Your personal philosophy is that it's best
to put them in jail before they commit any more purse
snatches, burglaries, robberies, and so on.

The checks don't belong to Rick, so it's a simple
matter of contacting the check owner to verify that they
are stolen. You drive the two blocks to the address on
the checks, but no one is home. The neighbors don't
know if there has been a burglary. Next stop is the
station to check the victim file. Nothing in the file.

You examine Rick's eyes under controlled
conditions, and he passes. Well, maybe he has a
warrant. You spend two hours trying to verify his
identity. That's unsuccessful also. You're pushing the
consent trip to the station at this point.

Without verifying the checks as stolen you cannot
charge Rick with possession of stolen property. Without
verifying Rick's identity, you cannot charge him with
lying to you or contact his parole officer. You're stuck,
so you have to let him go. You take a photograph of Rick

and drop him off near the station, at his request. You then drive back to your beat.

But you haven't given up yet. You still have his sister's residence to focus your investigation on. Just as you pull up, she drives up. You show her "Rick's" picture, and she identifies him as her brother, Randy "Sawed-Off" Featherly. A quick computer check shows he is wanted for a parole violation.

Next stop is the checkbook owner's residence. They also just got home from work. They were burglarized last week and the police were called, but no report was taken because they had not noticed anything missing. The checkbook had been kept atop a dresser but its absence wasn't noticed. You show them Featherly's picture, and they identify him as a past acquaintance.

You now have a good possession of stolen property case against Featherly, along with the warrant. You're hoping Featherly isn't too bright, and you make plans to hit his sister's house in the morning. The parole warrant will get you inside, and you'll tack on the possession charge when you book him.

Day two, 0700. You're knocking on sister's door, but you get no response. Without some evidence to indicate he is inside, you know you can't kick the door in. You approach a neighbor and show her Featherly's picture. She says she just saw him this morning at the house. Excellent.

It takes you one minute to remove a window pane and unlock the front door. Mr. Featherly is found taking a bath in an empty bathtub with his clothes on. Mr. Featherly is booked into county jail and is eventually sentenced to 36 months in prison for the stolen property charge.

HABITS OF THE ADDICT

As a street cop you have to "know dope." Habits of the street crook are the habits of a drug abuser. Addicts steal to support their drug habits. Gang members kill to defend drug sales or use drugs to fortify their courage for a drive-by shooting, prostitutes whore to buy a "fix," and juveniles steal to afford a weekend of "smoke" or use drugs to overcome the anxiety of adolescence.

Frequently, police officers are either afraid of drug arrests or think they are too much trouble. Their knowledge is limited regarding report writing, court testimony, the identification of drugs, or the symptomatology of drug use. Most drug-related arrests are self-initiated with evidence obtained through searches based on the observations of officers. A thorough knowledge of criminal law and criminal procedure is critical to this type of police work. This knowledge must then be articulated in the arrest report as well as the court testimony.

A book perspective handling drug arrests builds a minimal level of confidence in an officer. To be truly confident, the officer needs hands-on experience. An inexperienced officer needs to work with experienced officers to confirm suspicions and be guided through the report process.

The importance of an officer's confidence must be stressed, because dopers are the best liars, cons, and manipulators you will ever meet. They have been lying to family, friends, and cops for years. They are good at redirecting the focus of attention off themselves and onto a peripheral matter.

In police work, this manipulative ability allows them to successfully divert attention from their criminal behavior. For example, on a routine traffic stop the junkie exits the vehicle and approaches the officer. The officer directs the junkie to the curb, and the two of them discuss the traffic violation. The driver produces a license, and the officer issues the citation. The cop never gets close to the interior of the vehicle.

This deceptive maneuver was intended to keep the cop out of and away from the car. It could be because the car reeks of burning marijuana, the ignition is punched, or his hype kit is under the seat. Either way, the cop has been had. The solution is to understand he is trying to manipulate you. You can, however, turn the tables and use the conversation to your advantage. You can use the pretext of congeniality to obtain a consent search of the car or person.

You may also want to take back control at some point and direct him back for the registration or insurance papers. You can then conduct a plain-sight search of the interior of his vehicle without warning him that you are onto his game.

Critical to understanding the doper mentality—and this means the heroin addict, the "coke-head," and the "crystal freak,"—is knowing that they live for drugs. They spend every waking moment obtaining money for their next fix. Regardless of what time of day an officer contacts an addict, the addict will either be in the process of buying drugs, high on drugs, or stealing money for drugs. Keep this in mind when you contact an addict and his companions. Companions will be there to facilitate one of these

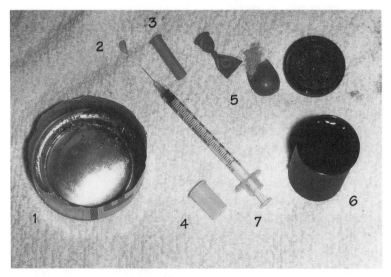

The components of a hype kit are illegal and provide probable cause for a trained officer to search: 1) aluminum can bottom used to heat the drugs mixed with water; 2) cotton used to filter out impurities while the heated mixture is drawn back into the syringe; 3) needle cap; 4) plunger cap; 5) cut toy balloon; 6) film canister with water; 7) barrel.

goals. Addicts do not have "friends"; they have acquaintances to get high with, steal with, or buy drugs from.

LANGUAGE

The language of the streets varies from subgroup to subgroup and from city to city. An officer needs to learn this language, not necessarily to converse with the criminal but to understand what may be said in a field contact or confession, or overheard on a concealed tape recording.

Common drug slang includes "brown," "boy," "shit," and "stuff" for heroin; "white," "girl," and "coke" for powered cocaine; "two-o," "rock," and "crack" for base cocaine; "lovely," "water," and "sherm," for PCP; and "meth," "crystal," and "go fast" for methamphetamine. Weapons may described as a "gauge" for a shotgun, "trey deuce" for a .32, and "shiv" for a prison-made knife. Convicts talk about having a "tail," which is the time left on parole. The examples are numerous, but all may not apply in any particular state or even the same city. Spend some time with a "friendly" source to learn a target group's language.

A mistake officers often make is to use street language inappropriately when conversing with criminals. Instead of seeing the "with it" persona the officer wanted to portray, the crook recognizes this mistake as a sign of weakness (the rationale being that if the officer is unaware of the proper use and meaning of this language, then he may have erred in the strength of the case against the suspect as well).

A key point in interrogating suspects is establishing in the mind of the suspect that you are in total control of the situation. The suspect should be convinced his life hinges on the decisions *you* make. You are then in a position to insist that he tell the truth; nothing else will do. However, if he senses weakness in your resolve or if you make a language error, the suspect will remain confident in a stonewalled position. Be careful using such language.

Establishing a profile of a doper allows you to focus your attention on those most likely responsible for criminal activity and to eliminate honest citizens from scrutiny. Fortunately, drug abusers often look like drug abusers. Besides the convict profile, drug addicts generally are pale and unkempt, wear long-sleeve shirts to cover track marks, are pale, and display the objective symptomatology of drug use.

The classic stereotype of the skinny, filthy heroin junkie, however, does not always apply. These individuals are consistent recidivists. Returning to prison or jail is a yearly event. These vacations from the streets allow the junkie to get "clean," eat better than on the "outside," and lift weights seven days a week. Do not automatically eliminate the well-nourished individual from your profile.

Keep in mind that dopers are usually unemployable due to their bizarre behavior patterns. They will be on residential streets when most employable individuals are working. A male in his thirties walking the streets at 1000 without a lunch pail or briefcase is suspect. Add a long-sleeve shirt and the avoidance of eye contact to this profile and a closer look is in order.

Each type of drug offers its own unique aspect of the doper profile. Working on a car at 0200 is a common activity for meth freaks, but not for sober citizens. The same is true for loitering at a street corner known for rock or crack cocaine sales.

Again, it should be emphasized, a profile match is not reasonable suspicion for a stop or probable cause for an arrest. It is simply a method to cull the street criminal from the herd.

THE CONTACT

After you have established a reasonable suspicion for the stop, approach the suspect. Focus on the hands and the objective symptoms of drug use. Use under-the-influence criteria to take the suspect into custody.

Now focus on determining what the suspect's scam is. Money for a habit is a primary need. Most are not that sophisticated in obtaining money; they usually resort to stealing or drug dealing.

PAGE _____ OF _____

11550 H&S — UNDER THE INFLUENCE OF A CONTROLLED SUBSTANCE SUPPLEMENTAL

PERSON ARRESTED (L. F. M)		DATE OF BIRTH	BKG. NO

CHARGES

I arrested _____ for being under the influence of a controlled substance

_____

_____

ORIGIN/PROBABLE CAUSE

REASON FOR CONTACT:

_____

_____

_____

_____

_____

_____

_____

_____

_____

THE SUSPECT EXHIBITED THE FOLLOWING OBJECTIVE SYMPTOMS:

OPIOID/HEROIN	STIMULANTS/AMPHETAMINE/COCAINE	PCP
☐ LETHARGIC MOVEMENTS	☐ HYPERACTIVITY	☐ AGITATED
☐ ABNORMAL WALK	☐ BAD COMPLEXION	☐ MUSCLE RIGIDITY
☐ SCRATCHING	☐ PROFUSE SWEATING	☐ ABNORMAL WALK
☐ SLEEPY LOOK	☐ SCRATCHING	☐ BLANK STARE
☐ NODDING	☐ OTHER	☐ UNUSUAL BEHAVIOR
☐ VISIBLE "TRACKS"		☐ OTHER
☐ OTHER		

I THEN CONDUCTED A FIELD EVALUATION AND HE EXHIBITED THE FOLLOWING OBJECTIVE SYMPTOMS:

☐ DRY MOUTH	☐ PARANOIA	☐ MEMORY LOSS
☐ CHAPPED LIPS	☐ NASAL RESIDUE	☐ HALLUCINATIONS
☐ COLD & CLAMMY SKIN	☐ NASAL IRRITATION	☐ PAIN TOLERANCE
☐ BRITTLE FINGERNAILS	☐ DRY MOUTH	☐ NON-COMMUNICATIVE
☐ NAUSEATED	☐ BAD BODY ODOR	☐ MOOD VARIATIONS
☐ OTHER	☐ STRONG THIRST	☐ OTHER
	☐ INSOMNIA	
	☐ OTHER	

Examination by _____ Witness by _____

Location _____ Lighting _____

Mechanical Aids: Flashlight/type _____ Pupil scale _____ Magnifier _____ Other _____

BREATH	EYES	PUPIL REACTION	PUPIL SIZE	
☐ ALCOHOLIC BEV	☐ BLOODSHOT	☐ NORMAL	Left Right	
☐ MARIJUANA	☐ WATERY	☐ SLOW	_____ _____	Suspect
☐ PCP	☐ DROOPY	☐ NO REACTION		Observer
☐ BAD BREATH	☐ OTHER	☐ HIPUS	**NYSTAGMUS**	
☐ OTHER		☐ OTHER	Left Right	
			_____ _____	Horizontal
				Vertical
			Contacts _____ Glasses _____	

CONTINUED ☐

Supplemental arrest form for use in under-the-influence cases. It was designed by the author and is used by the San Diego Police Department. The format ensures all legal issues and objective symptomatology is addressed by the arresting officer.

Besides common burglaries, dopers tend to specialize in crimes they have become relatively competent in, such as check forgery, use of stolen credit cards, pimping, and con games like "three-card monte."

When you come across a check forger, keep in mind the underlying motivation: drugs. This means you will be looking for the objective symptoms of drug use and searching for controlled substances, paraphernalia, and the remnants of past forged-check writing. These types of crooks are not first-time offenders. Most have been

PAGE _____ OF _____

ORIGIN/PROBABLE CAUSE (continued)

DESCRIBE MARKS:

Right side _____

Left side: _____

Tie off bruises noted? _____ Location _____

Location of Marks: Right Side

Location of Marks: Left Side

Based upon the above, the suspect was arrested for being under the influence of a controlled substance. _____

CHEMICAL TEST: ☐ Breath # _____ ☐ Blood # _____ ☐ Urine # _____

Taken at _____ By: _____ Disposition: _____

PHOTOS: Taken at: _____ By: _____ Disposition: _____

NARCOTICS/NARCOTICS PARAPHERNALIA: _____

EVIDENCE

INTERROGATION

Subject Admonished at this point: ☐ YES ☐ NO If "NO" Explain in Narrative.

Are you sick or injured? _____ Do you have any physical defects? _____

Do you take insulin? _____ Are you taking any medicine or drugs? _____

Are you under the care of a doctor or dentist? _____ Who? _____

Anything wrong with your eyes? _____ Have you ever had syphilis? _____

Have you ever had diabetes? _____ Have you ever donated blood? _____ Where? _____ When? _____

Where are you now? _____ What time is it? _____ (Actual time _____) Wearing watch: _____

What is the date? _____ What day of the week is it? _____

When did you sleep last? _____ How long? _____

Have you had anything to drink? _____ How much? _____ When? _____

What have you (smoked, snorted, injected)? _____ When? _____

How? (Pipe, cigarette, type of syringe) _____ Self injected? _____ Where on body? _____

Suspect's explanation of condition: _____

Explanation for refusal to take a chemical test _____

Disposition of Suspect: ☐ Jail ☐ CMH ☐ Hospital ☐ Other _____

REPORTING OFFICER	I.D. NUMBER	DIVISION	DATE - TIME	APPROVED

CONTINUED ☐

practicing for quite a while. Don't settle for a one-count check forgery case. Look for evidence, such as license applications, etc., leading to previous successful capers.

ARREST TRACKING

Building your expertise and confidence in narcotics arrests takes time and feedback on the arrests. Maintain a log of the subject's name, type of offense, and the drug suspected to be involved. Monthly, compare your log with the police lab report on the body fluid sample and its analysis of the controlled substance.

Make note of "negative test results" and multiple drug use. Three or more drugs may often be found in a subject's system. Morphine (metabolized heroin), cocaine, and THC (active ingredient in marijuana) are common results. Heroin and cocaine are often injected together in a combination called "speedballing."

Be particularly alert to results that totally conflict with your initial conclusion. A methamphetamine result is totally contradictory to a heroin conclusion. Re-evaluate your procedures to determine errors in observations or judgment.

FALSE NEGATIVES

Sample analysis of body fluids often does not coincide with the objective symptomatology displayed. A negative test result does not necessarily mean the officer erred in his conclusion; it may be due to a faulty laboratory testing procedure.

Common reasons for a false negative include the following: the urine sample was taken too early and the drug did not have time to get into the urine, the blood sample was taken too late and the drugs had been metabolized out of the system (drugs in the blood are metabolized quickly—eight hours), there was too little of the drug to be labeled a positive, the lab was incapable of testing for a particular drug (e.g., psylocybin or a "designer drug").

strategies in your particular county
and make adjustments for them. For
example, in San Diego County,
positive urine samples for PCP were attacked on the
claim that the PCP had been smoked days before and
was still in the system but the subject was not "under
the influence." The San Diego Police Department
adopted a policy of drawing blood from PCP suspects.
PCP has a half-life of only eight hours in blood, so a
positive sample can coincide only with the period the
suspect is actually under the influence.

Maintain a count of the number and type of arrests
you have made. This will be critical in establishing that
you possess more knowledge than the ordinary citizen.
A patrol officer with academic training, several drug
information seminars, and hands-on street experience
can qualify as a drug expert. His testimony and opinion
then allow the jury to draw conclusions based on his
expertise. A jury may or may not accept the expert
opinion, based on its evaluation of his credibility.

NARCOTICS PARAPHERNALIA

Immediate recognition of paraphernalia is a skill that
is useful in evaluating the type of person you are
dealing with and his conduct. It also offers immense
power in terms of the lawful search of the suspect,
vehicle, and residence.

Focus attention on the ashtray of a suspect's car.
Marijuana roaches are common plain-sight discoveries
that give access to the entire passenger compartment.
Cut-up toy balloons, small squares of aluminum foil,
and cellophane with a brown residue are sure signs of a
heroin user. Packaging materials vary from region to
region, so what is probable cause in one area might not
be in another. When writing the arrest report, be sure to
articulate the reason you believed the item was
paraphernalia, what its use is, and how you know this.

The parts of a hypodermic syringe are flags. This
includes the plunger, the barrel, the needle, the needle

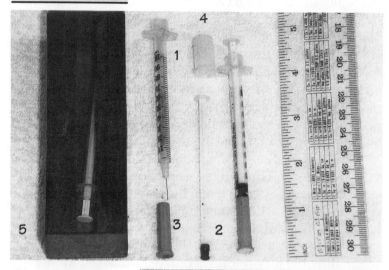

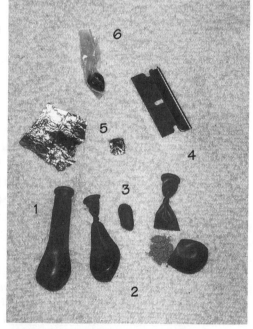

The various parts of a hypodermic syringe provide probable cause to search: 1) barrel; 2) plunger; 3) needle cap; 4) plunger cap; 5) syringe disposal unit. Carry syringe disposal units in the field to minimize the handling of syringes.

Heroin comes in two forms, either as a powder or as a tarlike substance. The powder is often packaged in toy balloons. 1) The powder is placed in the balloon, and 2) the balloon is then knotted and 3) rolled into a ball for carrying. 4) A sharp blade is then used to cut the balloon open. 5) "Tar heroin" is often packaged in small squares of aluminum foil or in 6) plastic. Remnants of such packaging material may provide a trained police officer with probable cause to search.

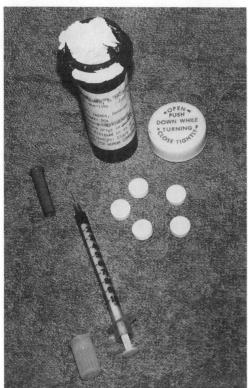

Pill junkies often combine pills and water in prescription bottles in preparation for injection. Treat the paste encrusting the bottle as a controlled substance (top left).

Rock cocaine is generally smoked in various types of glass pipes. This one is called a "straight shooter." 1) Straight shooter. 2) Bic lighter with flame setting on high. 3) Coat hanger used to clean debris from the pipe. 4) Glass vials and plastic Baggies are common rock cocaine containers (bottom left).

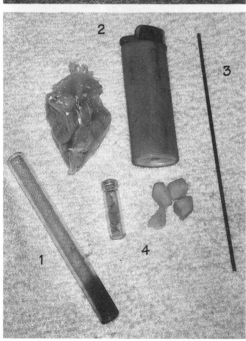

cap, and the plunger cap. Get used to looking for the individual elements. Cookers are less and less likely to be bent spoons and more likely to be scorched aluminum can bottoms or aluminum bottle caps.

Keep an eye out for film canisters and small glass viles. Both may contain drugs but are also used to carry water. The water is used to mix with the controlled substance prior to injection.

Pill bottles that prescribed medicine comes in should also draw an officer's attention, not only for the obvious reason that the pills may not be properly prescribed to this suspect, but for the use junkies have for them. Pills offer a substitute for heroin addicts when heroin is not available. The pills are ground up in the pill bottle and water added. This forms a paste which is then injected with additional water. An officer finding a paste-encrusted pill bottle should treat the paste as a controlled substance. The pills most commonly used are opioids, such as codeine, and, in the past, Talwin.

The injection of pills is also habit-forming and may become an exclusive method of getting high for some junkies. These "pill junkies" will inject as others do, but there is a distinct difference in their tracks. Because of the coatings and filling agents in the pills, the injection sites become ulcerated and infections commonly occur. The junkies' arms and hands swell up, taking on a very telltale appearance.

A bottle of 151-proof rum is a sign of base cocaine use. It is used to soak a cotton ball, which is then ignited and held up to the cocaine pipe. A 6-inch length of coat hanger is used to hold the cotton-ball torch. The rum is also used to clean the pipe. Watch for copper Brillo pad-type material used in the bowl of the pipe. Visit local head shops to determine the latest paraphernalia fads.

ASSET SEIZURE

Asset seizure is the wave of the nineties. Patrol officers should be cognizant of state asset-seizure

Head shops carry the latest in narcotics paraphernalia. You should make frequent visits to update yourself on the latest trends and to enhance your ability to recognize paraphernalia.

criteria or minimal asset value figures and seizure requirements.

Often important is whether the vehicle, motorcycle, or boat is paid for or at least has a large amount of equity. Be aware of paperwork indicating ownership, the amount of equity, and method of payment. A $60,000 Porsche with a $57,000 balance is usually not seizable. Save time by verifying with your asset-seizure team before impounding such a vehicle.

Rented or borrowed vehicles are usually not seizable. The rules provide for the protection of innocent third parties who are unaware their vehicles are being used for illegal activities. However, a vehicle previously encountered in a seizure situation may be seizable if the lawful owner was warned previously.

Large amounts of cash are, without question, desir-able. Be sure to keep from tainting the money prior to a "sniff" by carefully impounding it in a sealed plastic bag. A hit by a dope dog is usually all that is necessary to seize the money.

Mastering the world of narcotics encompasses most

of the desirable qualities of a good street cop. Work to gain expertise and experience in this area. Once you feel comfortable handling drug arrests, other areas of enforcement will come easily.

SUMMARY

1. Recognize junkies as the master manipulators. Use their pretext of congeniality to obtain consent searches.

2. Make an effort to learn local drug jargon, but be careful.

3. Establish a local profile of a drug abuser. Use it to focus enforcement action on abusers.

4. Identify the drug abuser's source of income.

5. Record and track your drug arrests.

6. Identify reasons for false negatives.

7. Learn to recognize narcotics paraphernalia and use this knowledge to establish probable cause for arrests and searches.

8. Understand and use asset-seizure laws to impound drug dealers' property and cash.

9. Visit head shops to learn about drug paraphernalia.

10. Talk to friendly users about their "habit."

0900, 3600 Ocean View Boulevard.

Officer: Good Morning, Lou.

Lou: Good morning, Officer Johnson.

Officer: What's up?

Lou: Nuttin.

Officer: You look a little tired.

Lou: Yea, my ol' lady kept me up all night.

Officer: I'm thinking you might have got down this morning.

Lou: Nah, I'm clean. I've been trying to kick.

Officer: Mind if I look at your arms?

Lou: Nah.

Officer: You have a couple marks here on your biceps.

Lou: Those? Those are from yesterday.

Officer: You sure?

Lou: Would I lie? You know me too good, Officer Johnson.

Officer: All right. Let me see your eyes.

Lou: Now, Officer Johnson remember, I'm nearsighted.

Officer: Don't worry, that won't affect the test.

The eyes usually clinch your decision on whether someone is under the influence of a controlled substance. Today you're pretty sure Lou is under the influence. You've known him for a year and have never seen him not under the influence. However, either because of multiple drug use or due to his age and lengthy habit, the pupils are not constricted to the point that you feel confident in arresting him. You explain your observations to Lou and let him go. He thinks you did him a favor and is grateful you were forthright with him.

1200, 3700 Ocean View Boulevard.

It looks like you'll be out of service for the rest of the shift. You have three adults in custody for being under the influence of PCP. They all reek of PCP, and you get a headache just talking to them. In Sammy's coat pocket, you find plastic sealing material and Sherman brand cigarettes. These items indicate Sammy is a PCP salesman.

You have searched Sammy and his companions thoroughly for the bottle of liquid PCP that goes along with this paraphernalia. You have no luck finding the PCP and figure it must be stashed at an unknown location. You're disappointed, but it's part of the game.

You hear a familiar voice.

Lou: Officer Johnson, Officer Johnson.
Officer: Yo, what up, Lou?
Lou: Come here.
Officer: You sure haven't got too far since this morning.
Lou: I'm just tryin' to stay out of trouble.
Officer: Something I can help you with?
Lou: Nah. This time I can help you. Check Sammy's shorts again, and thanks for being straight with me this morning.

Lou winks and slowly ambles away. You know what to do now. Sammy's taken into an examination room at the station. He is told to strip.

Under his scrotum is a bottle of liquid PCP, and your misdemeanor arrest is now a felony arrest.

Lou has just become a reliable confidential informant.

INFORMANT CULTIVATION

Cultivation of informants is important, but no one teaches you how to do it. That's because informants are the "bastard children of police work." Major cases would not be made without them, but they are so unpredictable and tainted by the criminal world they live in, police administrators fear this taint will rub off on young and tender patrol officers. Patrol officers are often warned not to handle informants but to turn them over to the detectives immediately.

Cultivating an informant may be as simple as giving one the impression a ticket has become a warning. The individual leaves with a sense of gratitude and relief. The next time you see him, pose some subtle questions regarding crime and criminals in the area. The subject senses a debt to you and provides you with the desired information.

A second method of cultivation may be an act of being courteous by offering a cigarette or a cup of coffee to someone who has approached you on the street. The informant lives in the underworld of crime. As a result, he does not have the same resources or knowledge the average citizen has in resolving various disputes. A patrol officer on the street often becomes his resource within the "system." Perhaps he has a complaint regarding a roommate or an opposing drug dealer.

Street Tip: Carry a pack of cigarettes with you, even if you do not smoke. Many of the street criminals (potential informants) you contact are heavy smokers. The gesture of offering a cigarette may be enough to establish a rapport. A cigarette can also be used to calm an agitated detainee or prisoner.

It is often difficult to determine who will be a "source" and who will not. During routine contacts with street people, ask them if they know of anything that would be of interest to you. Those interested in being informants will likely understand what you mean. This low-key approach may be enough to draw a potential informant out. Be careful with this approach; no one likes a "snitch" label, so avoid language they may interpret as being derogatory.

Street Tip: Put away your field interview (FI) pad and notebook when interviewing street people you know. If the subject's identity is established, forego the formalities of a field interview. Talk on a social level with these guys. Ask about known associates or the latest football game. Once you have departed, prepare a slip to indicate a change of address, clothing description, current associates, etc.

The purpose of a field interview is to identify the person (already accomplished), to arrest (not an issue here), and to gain street information. The first step in gaining such information is establishing a rapport with the individual. Once the interview book comes out, the subject knows this is business and will fall into a "police vs. us" mentality. You will not get any information this way.

The way to obtain information is to slowly build a rapport—not necessarily a friendship, but a relationship that allows him to feel comfortable talking to you. He then may—intentionally or unintentionally—reveal useful information. Keep in mind that regardless of the antipolice mentality these people often have, they still begrudgingly respect you.

From their early childhood, street people believed the police were the good guys and probably at one point in their lives wanted to *be* police officers. They still may obtain a thrill from associating with police. Cultivate this repressed desire to associate with police by not placing barriers to this association. Their anger toward police is usually generalized. Being personable with the guy will make it harder for him to hate and easier to open up.

Informants are motivated to work for money, to work off a beef, to work for revenge, or simply because they like the excitement of being around cops. Identify the motivating factor in each case and be prepared to use it to your advantage. If it's money, identify a department source to make it available. If it's to work a case off, identify the detective and DA assigned to the case and determine its status. Oftentimes a case is set to be dropped or may be reduced from a felony to a misdemeanor. Leaving the impression that this was your work will reinforce his debt to you.

When working with informants on a close or even casual basis, be careful not to "cross the line." No matter how strongly you feel personally about them, they cannot be trusted. Information you give them should be on a strictly need-to-know basis. Be particularly careful during war-story time and in casual conversations which may reveal other informants' identities or information regarding other investigations.

Street Tip: Run complete computer and identification checks on all of your informants. Informants may provide information to the police in order to remove suspicion from themselves for a variety of crimes. The most common situation a patrol officer will run across is an informant with a warrant. Be careful you are not being used so the informant can avoid arrest on the warrant, particularly felony warrants. If this is the case, carefully weigh the nature of the warrant against the value of the information provided.

Information to be gleaned from an informant need not be the solution to the "Brink's robbery." It may be the location of a particular drug dealer's stash on the street or a recently opened illegal after-hours club. These small exchanges of information can be used to build on your relationship until you're able to direct him to locate a particular criminal or organization.

CONTROL

Routine contact with the informant is important. It reinforces your relationship and provides a ready avenue for information exchange. However, a patrol officer should not expect to maintain the amount of control over an informant that an investigator would in an ongoing investigation. Due to their very nature, informants in ongoing investigations need a large amount of care and handling, including constant babysitting, handholding, and discipline. A patrol officer shouldn't expect to maintain this high level of control, but regular contact will work to some degree.

The use of a pager by a patrol officer can be invaluable in maintaining contact. This allows you to avoid the distasteful disclosure of a home phone number but still provides ready contact with the informant. Designated number codes for informants will help screen nuisance calls from the nonperforming nut cases attracted to this business.

The primary lesson for patrol officers in using informants is how to control them. They will lie to you, use you, and betray you if it will save their skins. Using, controlling, and learning from informants on this "lower" level of crime will prepare you to deal with them effectively on major operations. Treating them fairly but firmly is the key to handling informants.

A patrol officer has an opportunity to cultivate a string of informants while on the streets. Informants will increase in value when the officer moves into detectives. As a detective, the officer will have the resources and time necessary to utilize the informant's information fully. However, removing an officer from the streets to a detective's desk reduces opportunities to cultivate additional informants. While you're on the streets, don't waste this valuable opportunity, and don't ever trust an informant.

SUMMARY

1. Cultivation of an informant may be as simple as being courteous and friendly with street people.

2. Put your FI pad away when talking with known criminals (i.e., potential informants).

3. Identity a potential informant's motivation and learn how to appeal to it.

4. Give potential informants your pager number.

5. Never use derogatory terms in reference to other informants in front of informants.

6. Look at every contact on the street as an opportunity to cultivate informants.

7. Maintain regular, casual contact with all of your informants.

8. Run complete computer checks on *all* informants.

9. Don't trust any informant.

esidential burglary occurring now at Myrtle and Fairmont. Suspects last seen southbound on Fairmont in a blue Honda," your radio blares.

You're responding from 54th and Euclid, and experience tells you they're heading for the 805 freeway. Bingo, you spot them before they hit the on-ramp, and you and half of your division conduct a hot stop.

The suspects immediately yield, and the stop goes off without a hitch. The witness is called to the scene and identifies both suspects. The stolen property is recovered from the car. Before they're even booked, you're patting yourself on the back, wondering when you're going to get that commendation.

You still want to do everything right, and you know not to Mirandize the suspects right away or in each other's presence. On the drive downtown, you discuss the prospect of a high-speed chase with them. "If we had a 5.0 Mustang you would never had caught us," one suspect says. You notice a well-drawn black tattoo on one suspect's forearm, "Nice tattoo," you comment. "Thanks, I got it when I was in the navy," he replies.

These guys are cooperative, and you advise them of their rights separately. Both answer, "yes," that they understand their rights and, "no," they do not wish to talk. No problem, you think, you already have enough to convict.

Next step: "What's your name?" Their identifying information rolls off their tongues like they've said it a hundred times before. A quick computer check shows they are clean, just like they said. They didn't have any identification, but your sixth sense isn't kicking in.

Next stop, county jail. With their "clean record" and cooperative, nonviolent behavior, they're likely to be released on their own recognizance. So you think you've done a great job, and you can't wait for lineup to impress everyone with your street smarts.

Well, you blew it. They lied about their identities. These guys were "parolees at large" (PALs) with parole violation warrants out for their arrests. They are hard-core: hard-core heroin addicts and hard-core convicts. They can make even the best patrol cops jump through hoops.

RECOGNIZING THE CONVICT

From the beginning of any contact you should be anticipating the worst, that the suspect is hard-core and lying to you. The hard-core criminal is the one with extensive experience dealing with police officers, probation officers, judges, and the criminal justice system in general. They are usually cons, as in convicts, parolees or ex-cons.

They are good at handling the police. They know what to do and say to keep you in control (i.e., keep you from searching them, their cars, and their houses; investigating their identities; investigating the original call; etc.)

The Attitude

Your first clue as to whom you were dealing with was their "attitude." Remember the last time someone really made you angry, you spent a half hour looking through the municipal code for the section on washing a car in the street. Well, these guys know what happens when you upset a cop. They also know what happens when they give you what you ask for. The cop fills out the FI, ticket, and so on, and then leaves.

Convicts are programmed in the prison system to behave in an outwardly respectful manner toward law enforcement. This is due to the daily strict, regimented behavior patterns dictated by prison guards and the training they receive from older, more experienced convicts. Convicts know what aggravates and precipitates an aggressive investigation by a patrol officer. They attempt to placate the officer, thus circumventing this intense scrutiny.

Physical Appearance

The second warning sign was their physical appearance, in particular, the tattoo. A prison tattoo is a neon sign identifying the subject as hard-core. Prison tattoos are distinguishable from commercial tattoos by their lack of color. They are almost exclusively black or dark purple. They are often referred to as "black art tats." The tattoo is applied with a needle wrapped in thread that has been dipped in ink or with the sharpened barrel of a ballpoint pen. The needle or sharpened pen barrel is used to open up the skin and allow the ink to drain in.

Prison tattoos are most often of very high quality and serve several purposes. First is the covering of track marks. Convicts/junkies (most often one and the same) start off injecting in the arm opposite their dominant hand. The inner elbow offers the most accessible veins, and the arm is easily stabilized on a tabletop. As the veins in the inner elbow burn out, the injection sites move down the forearm and so do the tattoos. The most common tattoos in this area are the faces of women with

A sharp-eyed police officer should recognize immediately that this individual is a convict and IV drug user. The color of the tattoos ("black ink") just visible at the elbows indicate they are prison tattoos. The location of the tattoos at the inner elbow indicate their use to cover track marks (top right).

Convicts are often tattooed extensively. Don't settle for identifying the ones usually visible on arms or face. Have suspects remove their shirts and, under the appropriate circumstances, their pants. Chest, back, stomach, and leg tattoos are very popular in prison (bottom right).

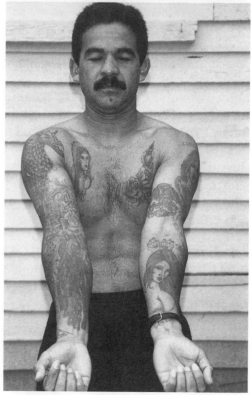

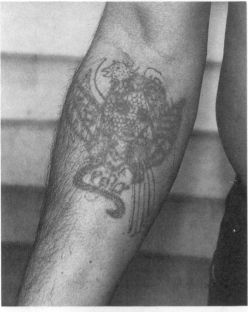

This original and rather crude tattoo is that of a woman's face. It is now in the process of being covered by a more expertly drawn bird with long feathers. Older tattoos are often covered by newer tattoos. Examine these new and intricate tattoos closely to determine the type of tattoo covered.

This individual has a number of tattoos that can provide some interesting insight. The rose at his left inner elbow is used to cover a small area used for injections. This indicates he is an IV drug user. The tattoos "Maria" and "Luisa" can be entered into a computer system for identification purposes. The roses on the belly were used to cover an old tattoo of his name. The skeleton warrior is a common prison tattoo theme.

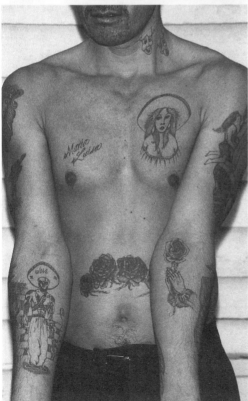

Tattoos on the face and neck are clear signs of having served time in prison. A tear drop tattoo signifies having served one prison sentence (top right).

The top tattoo on this arm is a prison guard tower. Such tattoos, as well as tattoos of barbed-wire-topped walls, spider webs at the elbows, and macho figures such as grim reapers and gang members are all common prison tattoos. They immediately identify the subject as a convict (bottom right).

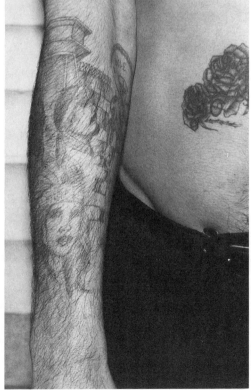

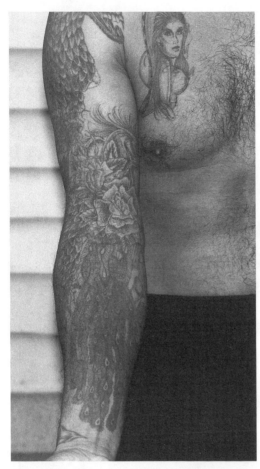

Extensive IV drug use results in scarring (tracks) of the veins. Intricate tattoos are then used to cover scarring. Common covering tattoos are peacock feathers, roses, and faces of woman with long hair. At the elbow of this arm are roses, and on the forearm are peacocks.

long hair, and peacocks with long feathers. They offer the most effective concealment for tracks.

A second purpose for tattoos is gang affiliation. Affiliation with a particular gang may be identified by nicknames, the name of the gang, or the convict's hometown. These tattoos may cover his entire chest, stomach, back, or legs.

A third purpose of tattoos is to cover old tattoos. Often juveniles will self-apply crude homemade tattoos to their biceps, hands, or forearms. This is usually a girlfriend's name or their own name (Mike Tyson has "MIKE" tattooed on his biceps). At the web of the hand, you may find a cross, dots, "love," or "hate" across the fingers. These homemade tattoos are often covered by a

Pay close attention to paperwork associated with street thugs during any contact. Paperwork is often a source of identification or offers a means to recognize the suspect as hard-core. In this case, the doodlings of a convict on prison stationery immediately identify him as hard-core.

more intricate prison tattoo. Pay close attention to heavily tattooed areas in order to identify the covered tattoo. It may help identify someone who is lying to you.

Most "tatted up" convicts wear long-sleeve shirts to cover tattoos and track marks. However, a dead giveaway tattoo is one on the neck or face. The classic teardrop tattoo under the eye or bluebird on the neck immediately identifies a suspect as a convict; be careful, convicts are very dangerous when their freedom is threatened.

Besides prison tattoos, convicts also develop physical characteristics and habits attributable to their life behind bars. Often they maintain short haircuts, wear long-sleeve blue work shirts buttoned at the collar, wear black work shoes, cover their heads with bandannas with the knot rolled under, sit on their haunches, or have buffed-out body-building physiques.

A curious aspect of their body-building behavior is the fact they rarely work their legs. Most of the weight lifting is dedicated to their upper bodies, hence the term "parolee legs" (skinny in contrast to a well-built upper body).

Habits

Two unique habits picked up in prison are eating positions and walking behaviors. A convict eating a meal looks like a pit bull guarding his food dish. He sits close to the plate and almost envelopes it with his arms in a protective stance. This habit develops out of the need to protect his food from other inmates. A convict walking the streets is not relaxed. He is almost as paranoid as an undercover cop. He constantly looks from side to side and about every 30 seconds will glance over his shoulder. This habit can be attributed to a life of crime and the fear of attack in prison.

Street Tip: Sometimes curiosity will drive a convict crazy; after a cop drives by he will sneak a peek. Watch your mirrors for this little peccadillo. This slip may point to a person you want to talk to.

MIRANDA

The third key to recognizing convicts is to notice the response to Miranda questions. The unsophisticated individual most often will want to talk to the police to give his side of the story. The careful but unsophisticated individual may be unwilling to talk to the police. He has learned that much from TV, but he will be less direct in refusing to waive his rights. He will respond with, "Should I talk?" or "Maybe I ought to talk to my lawyer first." The convict is more likely to be direct. "Yes" and "no" are his responses to the questions, "Do you understand your rights?" and "Do you want to make a statement?"

THE HEROIN CONNECTION

Once you have determined that you are dealing with a convict, be cognitive of his life's motivating force—drugs. One of the most overlooked aspects in the lives of the majority of convicts is heroin addiction. Unlike the current headline-grabbing drugs of cocaine and methamphetamine, heroin has not been transitory. It's been in this country for a hundred years, maintaining a relatively stable level of use. The drug is gentle to the human body in comparison with other illicit drugs because it's similar in chemical structure to pain-killing endorphins naturally secreted by the brain. Because of this similarity, the body does not react adversely to it. And the truth is, it feels "damn good." Heroin addicts are often lifetime junkies with minimal success at kicking it. Hence, they lead a lifetime of thievery.

CONTROLLING THE CONVICT

The key to handling convicts is to first recognize that you are dealing with a very intelligent and dangerous individual. The second is to not let on that you recognize him for what he is. Use his attempts at manipulation to your advantage. Use their facade of being good-natured to acquire their identifying information (some of it may be true), a consent search to examine his arms for tattoos or tracks, or a search of his person or vehicle.

An advantage to the street cop in dealing with convicts (parolees) is the control parole officers have over the convicts' lives. While a patrol officer does not necessarily have carte blanche to search a parolee (although he does with some probationers), his parole agent does. Upon identifying a convict, ask for his parole agent's name. Call the parole agent and advise him of the nature of the contact. You cannot ask to search the parolee. However, the parole agent may request that you search him and his residence in his stead.

Ask the parole agent if the parolee is "on the run" (hasn't shown up for periodic interviews or drug testing). The parole agent may be in the process of writing up a warrant for the convict's arrest but hasn't entered it in the computer system. Be aware that most parole warrants are not in local computer warrant systems but are in the federal NCIC system.

Street Tip: If the parolee is to be booked into jail, ask the parole agent for a "parole hold." This may be teletyped to the jail or hand-carried by the agent. A parole hold will prevent the parolee's immediate release and allow the agent time to revoke his parole.

One of the best sources of information on street life for the police officer is the convict. Sit down with a convict and talk to him about "hustling" money for "dope," "shit," "stuff," "chiva," etc. The lesson won't be free. It will cost you at least a pack of cigarettes. If you want to be a good street cop, however, you're going to have to learn from the best street thug, the convict.

SUMMARY

1. Covertly handle every suspect as if he were a convict.

2. Use a convict's attempts at manipulation to gain information and cooperation.

3. Play ignorant as to his status until it suits your purpose otherwise.

4. Examine all tattoos closely for tracks, names, and old tattoos.

5. Document all tattoos on arrest reports and field interview slips.

6. Pay close attention to suspects refusing to make eye contact.

7. A convict responds to the two Miranda questions with a "yes" and a "no."

8. Actively look for signs of drug use and illegal sources of income.

9. Use under-the-influence laws to target convicts.

10. Watch suspects closely for habits acquired in prison, such as manner of dress, physique, and speech.

11. Call the convict's parole agent.

12. Ask a convict to teach you about street life.

 ou're working a uniformed selective enforcement unit directed at street narcotics. It's the beginning of the afternoon shift, and you and your partner, Homer Stevens, are looking for action. You start off by hitting the hot spots in your area. You "swoop" on different locations hoping to catch the dealers off guard, forcing them to drop the drugs as you approach. It's still a little early for the drug swap meets to open, so you move quickly from one location to another quickly.

Forty-fifth and Logan shows some promise, and you cruise through the low-class liquor store's parking lot. You have never understood the neglect that allows such shops to decay to the point where you feel like washing your hands every time you come out with an overpriced orange juice. Homer recognizes a few of the homeboys and strikes up a casual conversation. The gangsters are animated and seem to have had their cages rattled.

Three Fingers Capone is on a friendly basis with Homer and outlines recent events. ("Three Fingers" is an apt nickname for Mr. Capone because it describes his right hand. Seems he and a 12-gauge shotgun had an abrupt meeting several months ago at the same street corner. Capone is a slow learner.) Three Fingers and friends have claimed alliance to a group of youthful miscreants. Apparently a rival group of social equals paid a courtesy call at 45th and Logan. They announced their dislike for Three Fingers and company and issued a challenge for a game of dodge the lead. Three Fingers and company declined the offer, as their game gear was unavailable.

Homer is familiar with local customs and the required protocol of such events. Due to the mutual hostility between rival teams, immediate access to game gear by challengers is a requirement. Homer concluded Three Fingers' rivals, the Neighborhood Crabs, were heavily armed.

Transportation for the Crabs was a 1967 white Cadillac with tail fins—a unique-looking vehicle and readily identifiable. Homer insists on visiting the Crabs' home field to check for some pregame planning sessions. You proceed directly to the "Neighborhood" and grid-search the residential streets. Thirty minutes into the search, the "ride" is located. Alongside are the Crabs, soaking up some liquid courage before the big game. The beverage of choice is Old English 800, a classic malt and barley mixture with strong social-stimulation enhancers but still affordable to even the most thrifty of gamesters.

Contact is made, and a lineup card is developed in case penalties need to be assessed. The vehicle is given a visual inspection, and a 12-gauge shotgun shell is spotted on the floorboard. This item indicates the game is for keeps, which requires a little stronger enforcement of the rules. The vehicle and players are given a thorough search for any illegal instruments of death, but no luck.

Check inside doors for concealed weapons and drugs by removing door panels.

So far everything has added up in Homer's analysis of the game plan. Three Fingers' description of the car matches, the challengers have been located and identified, the visitors are juicing up for the big event, and a shotgun shell has been found indicating the presence of weapons. The missing piece to the puzzle is the weapons.

Homer insists the Crabs would not have made the excursion to Mr. Capone's home field without weapons. So where are they?

Up to this point you have been along just for the ride, allowing Homer to exercise his expertise in such matters. It's about time you contributed to the case. You recall a piece of wisdom from the police academy: "Gangsters carry guns in the engine compartments of vehicles." However, out of the hundreds of cars you have searched, you have never found a gun in an engine compartment. You have never heard of anyone actually finding a gun there, either. In fact, just lifting the hood is a pain in the ass. The latches are often hard to operate, and you're almost guaranteed a trip to the local emergency room to scrub your grease-stained hands. Lately, this search is rarely used.

Up comes the hood and guess what? Three 12-gauge shotguns locked and loaded.

Street work does not require an in-depth knowledge of the social, economic, and emotional reasons for the establishment of gangs. What it does require is the ability to recognize the physical attributes of gang members, their criminal behavior patterns, and how you can use this information to arrest them.

As the above scenario demonstrates, knowing that the challengers would be armed, return to their home turf, and follow predictable crime patterns was essential in tracking them down. This chapter will focus on recognizing a gang member, identifying potential criminal patterns, and procedures to use in arresting them.

BLACK GANGS

In general, the focus of black gangs is social status

A personalized baseball cap is a popular gang identifier. "Trey Dog" is the subject's street name. "O.G." is a title of respect meaning "original gangster." "N-Hood" is the abbreviation for the name of his gang, Neighborhood Crip. "Rollin-40" means his gang claims all the streets in the 40s. "47th" is the particular street this gang member is from. "BK" stands for Blood Killer (the opposing gang being the Blood), and the X in the letter B indicates this Crip's disdain for the letter B, which he associates with the enemy. "Cuzz" is a nickname for Crips.

among peers and a facilitator for financial gain. They are less territorial than Mexican gangs. They are no less inclined, however, to defend "turf" over an incursion, particularly as it relates to drug dealing.

Colors

The primary black street gangs are Crips and Blood. The identifying characteristic of a member of one of these gangs is the color of his clothes. In general, Crips wear blue. Blood (also known as the "Piru") wear red. However, within each of these two general categories are smaller sets which usually align themselves with one group but have an individual color all their own. Sets are usually named after a street in their "hood" (neighborhood) or after the community itself, e.g., "Rolling 30s" "Eastside Piru," and "Logan Heights Red Steps."

The gangster may display his "colors" by wearing a particular color of jacket or cap. Currently popular are the jackets and baseball caps of professional sports teams. The L.A. Raiders and Kings (black) are the colors for Crips while the "Chicago Bulls" (red) are the colors for Blood. The colors may also be displayed by shoelaces, belts, and bandannas.

Street Tip: In years past the appropriate-colored bandanna was the identifier of choice. Now it is the baseball cap. Examine the cap for writing on the bill indicating gang affiliation and nicknames. Gangsters will often remove their caps when they spot the police. Search an abandoned stolen vehicle for caps left behind in the heat of the moment.

A make of shoes also is indicative of gang membership, in particular, the brand British Knight. The initials that appear on the shoes are "BK." The Crips have interpreted these initials to mean "Blood Killers." Wearing pants low to expose undershorts is also popular. It's called "sagging."

Hairstyles are not necessarily indicative of gang membership, but two styles are popular with hard-core members: ponytail braids and cornrows seem to be status symbols for some of the older ones, particularly those who have done time.

Language

The language of the gangster is unique. "Gauge" is a shotgun, a gun is a "gat," "trey deuce" is a .32, "deuce deuce" is a .22., "trey five seven" is a .357, and "trey eight" is a .38. To insult the opposing gang member, a Crip calls a Blood a "bug," and a Blood calls a Crip a "Crab." "Bust a cap" refers to firing a gun. "Take them off the set" means to kill them. "The set" is the streets. "Gaffle" is to be arrested and handcuffed. The police are called "one time" (one police car), "two time" (two police cars), and so on. Police are also called "Rollers" and "Babylonians."

Gang graffiti. From left to right: a list of the gang members' nicknames; "London"—the artist's name; "Brim"—a shortened version of the gang's name of "5/9 Brim" (brim as in the hats they would have worn years ago); "Blood Hound"—the nickname of the second artist, indicating 5/9 Brim is a subset of the Blood; "Steal$"—bragging that they are thieves; "OxG"—for "original gangster," a title of respect (the letter X replaces the period in gang graffiti).

West Coast Crip graffiti. From left to right: "Fucc the 1-Time"—"1-Time" is gang slang for a single police car, and Fucc is spelled with the letter "C" in place of the K, indicating the artist was a Crip; "Lil J-Nut"—artist's nickname; "Cuzzz" —slang for Crip; "W/Coast Crip"—"West Coast" is the name of the gang.

Blood graffiti. From left to right: "80$"—they claim the 800 block of the streets in the area (the S is turned into a dollar sign to indicate their interest in money); "Little Africa"—nickname of the gang and of the area they claim; "Piru$"—Piru is the street in Los Angeles where the Blood originated. It is used interchangeably with "Blood."

This graffiti is simple and clear. It marks the boundary of the "neighborhood Crips" (NH). Note the block-style lettering normally associated with black street gangs.

"O.G." refers to the words "original gangster." This is a title of respect. It may be earned by serving prison time, being a long-standing gang member, or performing a particularly nefarious crime.

A challenge to an unknown male is the word "cuzz," as in, "What up, cuzz?" if the challenger is a Crip. If the challenger is a Blood, the greeting is, "What up, Blood?" Using an inappropriate challenge is enough to start a fight or initiate a shooting.

Graffiti and everyday language reflect the animosity these gangs have for each other in the replacement of the letter "C" or the letter "B" in words used with the particular gang's starting initial. For example, a Crip will greet a fellow Crip by saying, "What it *ce* like?" instead of the traditional, "What it be like?"

Black gangsters tend to derive their nicknames from weapons they profess to carry or from the gangsters of the 1930s. For example, "Little Breakdown" refers to a type of shotgun and "Al Capone," of course, refers to a famous 1930s gangster.

Hand signs are used to identify the particular gang affiliation. The fingers are used to form the beginning initial of the gang. The fingers may also indicate a number. The number refers to the numbered street they identify with. A hand sign will be "thrown" (held up) to opposing gang members as a challenge.

Initiation into the gang may require a stated criminal act. It may be an armed robbery, a burglary, a drive-by shooting, or the vandalism of a police officer's private car. Street information pointing toward an initiation crime may indicate the investigation should focus on the "new" guys.

Drugs

The drug of choice for black gang members is rock or crack cocaine. Entire distribution systems within a neighborhood are often controlled by the area's ruling street gang. Violence between rival gangs is often over drug distribution rights in a particular area. Patrol officers' drug enforcement efforts (as described in

Mexican gang graffiti. This is a roster of gang members, but there is no identifying gang name. However, knowledge of the area will tell you which gang it most likely is. The fact that "Grumpy" and "Oso" are common Mexican street gang nicknames tells you the gang is Mexican. The script-type printing also indicates it is Mexican. The number 2 after "Oso" indicates he is junior to Oso 1 of the same gang.

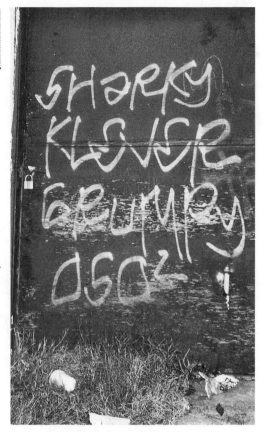

Chapter 11) serve as an effective gang suppression device. The San Diego Police Department conducted three separate drug operations in a two-year period, each targeting the Crips, the Blood, and a number of Mexican gangs. More than 300 gang members were arrested on felony drug charges (not the frivolous traffic warrant offenses that typically occur during well-publicized gang sweeps). The result was a definitive decrease in the number of gang-related homicides and assaults.

The fact is, arresting gang members for drug use, possession, and sales is a lot easier than preventing a shooting. Since most gang members are involved with drugs, the common-sense approach and the one proven effective (at least in San Diego) is to attack gang violence through drug enforcement.

Market Street gang graffiti. "Big"—means they're tough. "Mkt St"—abbreviation for Market Street and the name of the gang. "Mr. Byrd"—street name of artist. "Mr. Woody 2"—street name of second writer (the number 2 indicates there are two "Woodys" in this gang, and he is younger or less experienced than number 1). "Eme St"—Eme is Spanish for the letter "M." The white graffiti has been crossed out by an unidentified person who painted the word "Suck."

This graffiti was done by a subset of the Mexican Market Street gang called the "Alley Boyz." The number 13 refers to the letter "M," the thirteenth letter of the alphabet and the first letter in Market Street. Subsets are common. The names are a roster of "Alley Boyz" gang members; rosters are very common. Patrol officers should gather this type of intelligence information for use in future investigations.

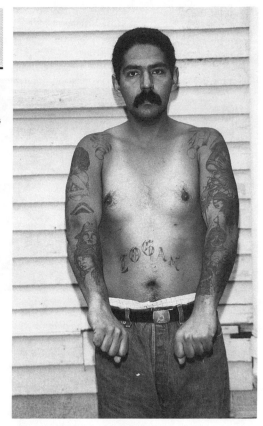

Tattoos are often used for gang identification. The tattoos on the shoulder are the letters "S" and "D" for San Diego. The "Logan" tattoo on the stomach identifies him as a "Logan Heights" gang member, which is a San Diego Mexican Street gang.

MEXICAN-AMERICAN GANGS

Clothing

The uniform of choice for Mexican-American gangs is a long-sleeve Pendleton shirt buttoned at the collar, baggy tan or black pants, and a white T-shirt. Bandanas are popular. They are worn low on the forehead just above the eyes and may also be carried hanging out of a pants pocket. The color designates the gang.

Language

Mexican-American gang members tend to gain nicknames from their physical appearance: "Sleepy," "Flaco" (skinny), "Huerto" (light complexion). Their physical appearance as it relates to animals is a particularly popular source of nicknames (e.g., "Oso"

[bear], "Spider," and "Mousy"), as is a personality characteristic (e.g., "Clown," "Smiley," and "Grumpy").

Gang graffiti can be an important source of information. Common graffiti will be the name of the gang followed by the nicknames of members. This information can verify the membership of suspected members. Gang members use tattoos to identify the gang they "claim" and their nicknames.

Street Tip: Graffiti can also signal problems between two particular gangs. For instance, if a gang's name has been crossed out and another written beside it, this is considered a challenge to the crossed-out gang. Even more troublesome is when the name of only one member of a particular gang is crossed out. Next to the crossed-out name is written either the name of the rival gang or a rival gang member's name. This indicates that the crossed-out member has been targeted by an opposing gang and is in definite danger.

Drugs

Besides marijuana, the most popular drugs of choice among Mexican-American gang members are PCP and heroin. Liquid PCP is placed on marijuana and smoked as a "joint" of "lovely." Heroin, primarily "tar" heroin, is popular with older gang members. In fact, extensive heroin use is a common factor leading to the user's disassociation with the gang. Gang activities tend to interfere with the addict's never-ending quest for dope money.

ORIENTAL GANGS

Increasing immigration of a number of Asians within the last decade has resulted in a proliferation of Oriental street gangs. The nationalities include Filipino, Viet-namese, Laotian, and Cambodian. These gangs have taken to emulating black gangs. They align themselves with "Blood" or "Crips," dress similarly, and use similar street language.

Two groups are considered archenemies. The Lao-

Oriental street gang graffiti. "OKB"—stands for "Oriental Killer Boys," the name of a Laotian street gang. A roster of members follows: Mr. Kiki Boy, Cuyamaca, Boy 13, and Loko 2. Laotians align themselves with the black street gang the Blood (or Piru). They therefore do not like "Crips" or the use of the letter "C;" thus, the letter "K" is used in "Loko."

tians and the Cambodians have brought long-standing feuds from their homelands to the States. They do not mingle. The Vietnamese are often the dominant gang due to their numbers, sophistication, and long history of gang involvement.

Orientals tend to victimize their own, and due to a cultural bias of the victims, they tend to avoid the police. Extortion, residential robberies, and car theft are their crimes of choice. They seem to prefer 9mms, .45s, and assault weapons as their guns. Routine practice with their firearms is a habit distinguishing Oriental street gangs from other street gangs.

WHITE GANGS

White gangs tend to form around the "skinhead" movement, the use of drugs, and bikers.

Often confused with the graffiti of street gangs is the work of "taggers." Taggers are youths who simply like to see their "mark" in public. To differentiate between the two kinds of graffiti, first look for a gang name. In this case, there is none. Second, gang members use traditional gang nicknames such as "Insane," "Capone," "Spider," and "Smiley." Taggers use unusual names such as "Sonek," "Tron," and "Ack," or simply their own initials.

Skinheads

Skinheads derive their name from having actually shaved their heads. They profess a racist philosophy and align themselves with neo-Nazis. They focus on intimidating minority groups, in particular gays and Jews. Certain groups may also dabble in the occult. "Devil worship" and animal sacrifices may play a role in these in gangs.

Skinheads wear black or red combat-style lace-up boots. The pant legs are rolled above the boot. Green U.S. Air Force jackets are also worn. White supremacy tattoos are popular.

Graffiti and tattoos may be swastikas, two lightning bolts (an identifier of the World War II elite German unit, the *SS*), and the initials "SWP" (Supreme White Power). Examples of Satanic tattoos include three dots at the web of the hand, three 6s (666), and a pentagon (a five-sided star). Each of these tattoos represents the sign of Satan. Tattoos on the palm of the hand are common.

The crimes of skinheads usually consist of senseless beatings of individuals on their hate list, vandalism of targets' buildings and property, and graffiti.

Stoners

A second category of white gangs is "stoners." They are usually high schoolers or not much older. Their preoccupations are smoking marijuana and, to a lesser degree, using methamphetamine and cocaine. Their graffiti consists of slogans such as, "Do Bongs" (smoke marijuana from a water pipe) and "Do Rails" (snort methamphetamine).

Their crime of choice is residential burglaries. They usually steal cash and items easily converted to cash by the unsophisticated thief.

Street Tip: Stoners are often in possession of paraphernalia associated with smoking marijuana. This paraphernalia includes pipes, cigarette rolling papers (Zig-Zags), film canisters, breath fresheners, and eye drops. Film canisters are used to carry the dope. Breath freshener is used to eliminate the odor of marijuana. Eye drops are used to "get the red out" (red eyes being an objective symptom of marijuana use). Possession of such paraphernalia is indicative of a stoner. A casual user will not usually walk around with these telltale objects. Keep in mind a stoner is often addicted to marijuana. Yes, marijuana is addictive—and expensive. Hence, theft becomes a source of funds for this addiction.

Bikers

The "Big Four" of the outlaw motorcycle gangs are the Hell's Angels, the Banditos, the Outlaws, and the Pagans. In addition, there are hundreds of other, smaller gangs, which usually align themselves with one of the larger ones. These gangs are organized crime. They have

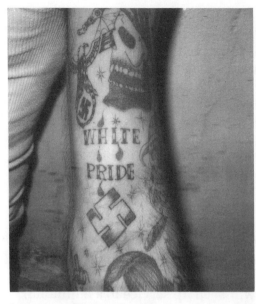

The tattoo of an Aryan Brotherhood prisoner. Prison tattoos on whites often focus on white supremacy themes. Often there is a Nazi theme as well, as evidenced by the swastikas.

bylaws, officers, bank accounts, cooperation agreements, and enforcement policies. The clubs are supported by any number of criminal enterprises, including murder for hire, drug manufacturing and sales, and auto theft.

These organizations are sophisticated and use a number of different types of legitimate businesses as fronts, including limousine rentals, motorcycle parts shops, and tattoo parlors. Clubs have any number of chapters in various states as well as foreign countries. Chapters are often called upon to support the parent organization in various crimes. Prominent is the hiding out of fugitive members who belong to other chapters.

Membership into such clubs is strictly regulated. The first level is the "hang-arounds" or wannabes. These are general club gophers. They are also a source of information, as their loyalty to the club may not yet be solidified. The next category consists of "prospects." They are allowed to wear a club's "colors" (a jacket with the club colors or an area rocker on it), but the jacket is missing the club logo. For instance, within the Hell's Angels, the prospect is allowed to wear the "rocker" which identifies the club chapter, but he can not wear the "death head" logo. After a period of initiation, the prospect is then voted in or out by the local membership.

This initiation process is lengthy to avoid infiltration by police and to test the mettle of the prospect. As a consequence, you should recognize any new face as being out of the ordinary and possibly an out-of-state fugitive taken in by a friendly chapter.

Bikers know the rules of the streets. They are often career criminals with a sophisticated approach to the police. Feigned respect for the police is the norm. However, an officer may run into trouble when dealing with a prospect, who may be required to assault an officer to qualify for gang membership. Furthermore, a veteran member may take exception to what he feels is "poor treatment." Never let your guard down, but understand these guys are not dumb and will play the game most of the time (they won't resist, will provide identification, and will keep lip service to a minimum).

A common identifying characteristic of outlaw motorcycle gangs is that they ride American-built motorcycles exclusively, including Indians, Harleys, and Triumphs. Also, hard-core bikers look hard-core. They wear Levis. Their footwear consists of well-worn black leather boots. A knife in a sheath is common. A large leather "biker" wallet with a chain attached is carried in the rear pants pocket. In states with helmet laws, riders often wear half-helmets, which cover the head to the ears and are usually black. Some law enforcement agencies do not believe these comply with current helmet laws and have resorted to citing riders who wear them for noncompliance with helmet laws and impounding the offending helmet as evidence. In states without helmet laws, no helmet is worn but a bandana might be. Black-framed "Easy Rider"-type sunglasses are popular.

An area overlooked by patrol officers with regard to bikers is their common use of passenger vehicles for transportation. They are not always on a "hog." Common biker vehicles are older El Caminos and Rancheros, Corvettes, and vans. Watch for the Harley-Davidson wing decals on the rear window to key you in to what you may be stopping. These vehicles attract less attention than the motorcycles and are used for drug,

Biker gang's colors (front). "13"—M is the 13th letter of the alphabet and the first letter in the word marijuana. "DFFL"—"Drugs Forever, Forever Loaded." "AFFA"—Angel Forever, Forever Angel." "1%er"—bikers often consider themselves the 1 percent of the world that just does not "give a shit." In the bottom left corner is the logo of a brand of cigarette rolling papers used for smoking marijuana. "DAGO"—stands for San Diego. "69"—mutual oral sex.

Hell's Angels colors (back). "Berdoo"—San Bernardino, California. "MC"—motorcycle club. (The bottom rocker changed to the state of the chapter in the early sixties.)

weapons, and stolen property transportation.

Enforcement Tactics

Outlaw bikers are criminals and generally do not share the work ethic of the population at large. Their motorcycles are usually 1950s and 1960s models requiring quite a bit of maintenance. Poor work habits and an aging motorcycle combine to create a moving equipment violation. Equipment violation enforcement is a good way to contact and get to know the locals.

Learning the identities and habits of local members should be a goal of the street cop. In any organized investigation of such clubs, detectives need basic information such as club hangouts, membership roles, current photographs, and identities of front organizations. The street cop is often in a good position to obtain this information.

Street Tip: A patrol officer is in a good position to apprehend fugitives "laying low" with a friendly chapter. Outlaw bikers generally have a large number of tattoos. These tattoos may identify which chapter they belong to and their names. A new face among local members should be a flag as to a fugitive biker and his tattoos a start in identifying him.

Drugs

Bikers' drug of choice is methamphetamine. Be conscious of the objective symptomatology of this stimulant, including rapid speech, continual movement, dilated pupils, dry mouth, and perspiration. Paranoia is an objective symptom of stimulant use and manifests itself in the obsessive need to be armed. Never let your guard down with these guys and always generate probable cause to search their person or vehicles for contraband.

* * * * *

Whether it provides the courage for a drive-by

shooting or an escape from everyday

life, drug use among all gang members is common. Strict enforcement of under-the-influence laws is a great gang-suppression device. Mandatory jail sentences in some states guarantee these guys will be off the street for months. A common condition of probation for such offenses is a search-and-seizure waiver. If you have a gang problem in your area, heavy under-the-influence enforcement is one solution.

Street Tip: In addition to search-and-seizure waivers, common conditions of probation for gang members are that they not associate with known gang members, not wear gang-related clothing, and stay away from gang hangouts. Violating one of these conditions is a bookable probation-violation offense. Become familiar with these probation conditions and to which members they apply. Probation departments often supply lists of known gang members and their conditions of probation. Carry this list with you.

Keep yourself current on ongoing rivalries between local gangs. During routine contacts with gangsters, ask about recent drive-by shootings and assaults. They may drop the name of the responsible gang or the shooter's name or nickname. This information may be enough to confirm other street information and lead to a photo lineup with the victim or other investigative follow-ups.

Being aware of rivalries allows you to plan a response to an attack on a targeted gang. Knowing who the likely suspect gang is points you to stake-out routes into its territory as the members return from the shooting. This knowledge also lets you focus on a specific list of gang members and their vehicles. You can then make a search through your gang file of the membership roles for the specific vehicle and owner.

Gang territories are often divided by particular streets. Appearance in a rival's territory is a challenge. A street cop should be aware of the boundaries of gang territories in the area and the style of dress for the local gang. Patrol officers should be adept at recognizing a suspect as a gang member and knowing whether he is out of his territory. Gang members are very aware of gang boundaries, most having grown up in a particular area. The appearance of an outsider wearing his colors in another's territory is intentional and potentially deadly.

SUMMARY

1. Learn to recognize the color and type of clothing associated with various local gangs.

2. Examine gang members' caps, paperwork, and tattoos for gang affiliation.

3. Learn to read gang graffiti.

4. Keep track of your hard-core gang members and learn their addresses, nicknames, tattoos, and companions.

5. Learn the local gang language.

6. Take lineup quality photographs of gang members for your department's files.

7. Separate witnesses to a gang assault before and during interviews.

8. Out-of-state bikers are often fugitives. Work to establish their true identities.

9. Use narcotic laws and probation violations for gang enforcement.

10. Keep up-to-date regarding various gang rivalries by their graffiti and through conversations with gang members.

11. Learn the boundaries of the various gangs.

CHAPTER 11

SPECIAL
ENFORCEMENT
TACTICS

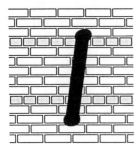

t's 0300 and you are bored stiff. No
one's on the streets. You've checked
all the parks, and the radio is dead.
You're not hungry because you've
already powered down a Denny's
Grand Slam breakfast. You're fighting the impulse to do
some eyelid checking, so you head for the station. You
don't know why, but it's better than drifting off into a
telephone pole.

You notice the green glow of a computer terminal as
you amble down a hallway. Then you have an idea. What
has Joe the Junkie been up to? You hit a few keys and
wham . . . burglary warrant worth $25,000 pops up. No
kidding, and you just happen to have seen him in front of
his mother's house last week. The next thought is, night
service? Sure enough, it's endorsed for night service.

Now you're rolling. You wake up Sarge, who is

passed out behind the day-old sports section of the "Daily Planet" and run the idea by him. He's a little embarrassed at being caught napping, so he's receptive to your idea of nabbing "Old Joe." He calls a meet for three other officers, and the five of you lay out the game plan. Two will take the perimeter and three for possible entry. You know you can't go kicking in mom's door based on what you have now. You know you need at least a reasonable suspicion to believe Joe is inside before you do that. However, there is nothing that says you can't go do a little 4 A.M. "knock and talk." Three things are likely to happen: Mom slams the door in your face, mom snitches off Joe, or Joe flushes out like a covey of of quail (the reason for two officers on the perimeter).

You call the marshal's office before you leave the station, and they verify the warrant is valid. The plan goes off like clockwork. Mom answers the door and before you give your speech, there's Joe, half-naked and in plain sight, sleeping on the living room couch. Legal entry is no longer a problem, and Joe is in handcuffs without a fuss.

Everyone is pleased at how the arrest went off. The gray matter begins to ponder the notion, "Why don't we do this every night?" So your squad develops a "Graveyard Warrant Service Program." Each member begins to select past criminal acquaintances to run for warrants. A formal procedure is established to ensure the arrests are conducted by the book. Night service requirements are checked, the marshal's office is called to verify the warrant, computer checks are run to identify the suspect's possible location (it is often other than what is on the warrant), and officers are briefed as to what constitutes a reasonable suspicion that a suspect is inside a particular residence (e.g., his vehicle parked in the driveway, witness statement, phone call to the house asking for him).

Additional computer checks are run to examine possible threats such as other criminal residents, warrants for those occupants, search-and-seizure waivers for the target as well as other occupants, and firearms registered to the occupants. Guidelines are established as to the nature of the

warrants to be served: no traffic warrants; only serious misdemeanor and felony warrants will be served.

A regular pattern develops. Clear all calls by 0300 (background checks are finished the morning before, calls to the marshal at 0330, on the road and swooping by 0340. Half the arrests are for the warrant suspects; the other half are for companions or subsequent contraband discoveries. Graveyard rolls by, and you actually enjoy going to work.

A warrant service program is just one example of the self-initiated proactive police work a "street cop" can utilize to target the hard-core criminal. These guys are not going to come to you. You have to dig for them where they live and hang out. The warrant program targets them in their residences; the following strategies target them both at home and on the streets.

STREET NARCOTICS SALES

Street narcotics sales result from several drug dealers occupying a street corner and servicing pedestrian and drive-up customers. The dealers operate in an open manner and will often boldly solicit passersby. The focus of enforcement action will be possession, possession for sale, and under-the-influence charges.

At the street level, drug dealers are often junkies. They sell enough to keep themselves high. They are almost continually under the influence. This condition presents ready cause for the "stop" and subsequent arrest. The patrol officer should focus on this behavior and watch for the objective symptoms of narcotics use.

Effective enforcement action against these dealers often requires the assistance of several officers. Movement into a targeted area should be coordinated over a tactical frequency as you approach. "Swooping" on a street corner resembles the light switch being thrown on a cockroach-infested kitchen. Within a minute the corner will be vacant. Some will run, others will amble away, and a few may even stay put.

A noncriminal suspect running from the police is not committing a crime. Unless you have reasonable suspicion to stop him, keep your hands off. If he's caught with the drugs still on him, the arrest will have been improper. Let him go, and focus on the

Street-level drug dealers commonly conceal their drugs nearby. Check likely hiding areas during field interviews.

one who is attempting to blend into the woodwork. He's the one moving slowly but deliberately away from you. He will be holding. His dope

will be in his underwear, the sleeves of his jacket, his socks, or his mouth. If this guy is under the influence, then you have the probable cause to stop, arrest, and search him.

If he is not displaying the objective symptoms of narcotics use, you must have a reasonable suspicion he has committed a crime (see Chapter 1). You will then need probable cause to search him.

The ones still hanging out at the scene may simply be bold or their stashes are not on them. They have either hidden them nearby or dropped them upon your approach. The key in hitting such a location is watching the hands of the suspects. The drugs will be in a potato chip bag, milk carton, or scrap of paper. As soon as you're spotted, the trash is dropped to mingle with the other garbage. The dealer will then move away from it but stay close enough to keep an eye on it. Routinely checking trash and likely hiding places will often result in the recovery of drugs. Check in water meter boxes, under rocks, beneath chunks of removable grass, and so on.

Mouth holding presents a problem for patrol officers because there is no clean way to recover the drugs. If the suspect hasn't swallowed them by the time the officer has discovered he is holding, the suspect will then start to swallow. The officer will immediately apply the standard "Darth Vader" death grip on the suspect's throat. It will then be a matter of luck whether the dope gets spit out or swallowed.

Street Tip: A suggestion is to bend the suspect over at the waist. This forces him to swallow "uphill." Keep in mind the force used to recover physical evidence (the drugs) is limited to that which would not "shock the conscience of the court."

Watch for transactions occurring between a dealer on foot and a drive-up customer. Don't dismiss this activity as an innocent conversation between friends. As you drive up, the conversation will conveniently end, and the customer will drive away. Assign an officer to stop the car away from the area. Questioning a scared customer may result in the probable cause necessary to arrest and search the dealer.

Street Tip: Conceal yourself in a location overlooking the area in which drug sales are taking place. Use binoculars to identify the dealers and the location of their stash. Watch several transactions occur to establish a particular dealer's dominion and control over his drugs. Once you have established that a particular stash belongs to a particular dealer, move in and detain the dealer, locate the drugs, and arrest him.

RESIDENTIAL DRUG SALES

Patrol officers often become aware of residential drug sales through radio calls and informants. Your overworked narcotics unit may be unable to handle the problem. Drug houses are more than a quiet source of narcotics. They become the focus of neighborhood complaints because of loud parties, shootings, and excessive foot and vehicle traffic.

The first steps an officer should take in the investigation of a drug house is to identify the owner or occupants. An address check through the county recorder's office will reveal the owner's name. Running license plate numbers of vehicles in and around the house and calling the water and gas company may identify the occupants.

Add the house to your list of places to be visited frequently. Look for various code violations and take enforcement action. A vehicle blocking a sidewalk, a dog off leash, and abandoned refrigerator with its door in place (they must be removed) are examples of typical drug house violations.

Make your presence known if you happen to be writing parking tickets for suspect vehicles. Turn your

Motels are often used for drug dealing, hide-outs, and prostitution. Routinely patrolling the parking lots and reviewing the sign in logos can lead to quality arrests.

radio up to gain attention. The subjects will first watch to see what the police are doing there. They may be paranoid enough to flush the dope. After watching you for awhile, if it appears you are only writing a ticket, they may approach to challenge the ticket. Take this time to have them identify themselves.

Once you have identified the occupants, run complete criminal computer checks on them. Look for arrest warrants, search-and-seizure waivers, and parole status. You may be able to get the parole officer to help in addressing the problem. Keep in mind that if you take action, these guys are paranoid and dangerous. It may be time to call in SWAT to assist in the arrest warrant entry.

MOTELS

The use of motels for drug sales is very common. An officer working an area with low to moderately priced motels should make an effort to establish a relationship with motel management. First, they are a valuable source of information, and second, they may be involved in illegal activities themselves.

Brief management on the "profile" of a drug dealer using motels. Such dealers pay in cash, are local residents and not visitors, make numerous phone calls, refuse maid service, request particular rooms at the back of the motel, and have frequent and numerous visitors.

Research your local ordinances applying to motels. Learn whether or not the register must be supplied for inspection and if identification is required upon registering. Make frequent motel parking lot checks for suspicious-looking vehicles (parked as if an attempt is being made to conceal them, punched out trunk and door locks, fit the profile of local drug vehicles, etc.). Frequently local dealers will use rental registration. Do not overlook them in your patrol of the lots. Run warrant and stolen checks on suspicious vehicles. If anything suspicious comes up, contact the management to determine ownership of the vehicle and the room they are in. If your suspicions appear to be warranted, apply the standard proactive enforcement stance of arrest warrant service, search-and-seizure waiver, consent, etc. Then make contact with the occupant of the room.

KNOCK AND TALK

If your efforts at identifying and arresting the residents are unsuccessful or only partially successful, you may want to do a "knock and talk." This means you walk up to the front door and knock. You apprise the occupant of the nature of the complaint you have received. You then ask to come inside and discuss it.

Critical in this initial contact is a low-key approach and demeanor. Although most complainants are accurate in their deduction of what is occurring, sometimes the complaint is false because it was made in error or out of spite. You do not want to anger an innocent person and you do not want to alienate the guilty.

The object of the contact is to gain consensual entry to the residence for a plain-sight observation, to identify the occupants, to seek a consent search, and to resolve the complaint. Once the person has been advised of your purpose, ask to search ("look around") the house. Offer to be escorted and explain you will be neat in your tour.

Knock and talk is a fairly successful method in handling such complaints. The dopers are caught off guard and find it difficult to refuse a well-stated request to search. Keep in mind you're on the premises at their discretion, and when they slam the door in your face or tell you to leave, then you must stop immediately and depart.

A word of caution on such investigations: depending on your department policy you may want to contact your narcotics unit, a county-wide task force, or the feds to ensure you do not compromise an ongoing investigation. This problem does occur occasionally, and most agencies have an index indicating what residences are being investigated and by whom.

SHOOTING GALLERIES

Another aspect of drug houses is the "shooting gallery." A "shooting gallery" is a house or apartment used on a regular basis by intravenous drug users to inject themselves. While snorting or smoking narcotics is openly accepted in some circles, injection is usually conducted in semiprivacy. Hence the need for "shooting galleries" among a largely transient population of junkies.

Shooting galleries are often abandoned residences taken over by addicts. They are usually in exceptionally poor physical condition and present a hazard to children and the neighborhood. A lasting solution to such a shooting gallery is to notify the city building inspection department, health department, and fire department. These entities can force an absentee landlord to clean the place up.

Street Tip: Shooting galleries are the source of

numerous abandoned syringes. These present an obvious hazard to children and your fellow police officers. Obtain a needle disposing device from your local hospital and carry it with you to the house and destroy the needles on site. This reduces the additional handling of the disease-infected needles required in transporting them to the hospital for disposal.

BARS

Neighborhood bars may be a source of narcotics or provide an outlet for fencing stolen goods or gambling. These bars may come to the attention of patrol officers through radio calls regarding drug use, fights, and shootings. Bars are regulated by the vice squad and Alcohol Beverage Control agents. Because of staffing constraints, a patrol officer may find it necessary to deal with problem bars.

Often the illegal activity, whether drug sales or the interrelated crime of fencing stolen property, will be centered in adjacent parking areas, residential streets, or the bar itself. Make it a practice to check these areas as you travel from one "hot spot" to the next.

There are myriad vice laws which extend the powers of the police behind the bar itself. Become familiar with the ones you can and cannot enforce.

Through nuisance-bar regulations, a bar can be shut down by Alcohol Beverage Control agents. You can get the ball rolling by compiling a number of reports on the complaints regarding the bar. If you make an arrest or take a crime report related to the bar, forward a copy to your vice unit and the Alcohol Beverage Control Department.

Problem bars usually become that way because the owner or employees actively participate in criminal activity that takes place there. Keep this in mind when handling a call and make an effort to properly identify bar owners and employees. You can then hit the computer looking for warrants and search-and-seizure waivers.

Parks become a focal point of illegal activity because of the criminal's desire to avoid public scrutiny. Parks offer some seclusion from such attention and often become drug distribution centers and gang hangouts. Daytime brings a combination of legitimate and illegal use. During the night, visitors will tend to be the criminal element.

Generally, parking lots and vehicles will be the center of the illegal activity. Place your attention on them when you enter. Watch for the vehicle that departs immediately upon your arrival. Focus your enforcement action on this vehicle. Once in the park, actively seek a legal basis to contact people in their vehicles.

Start foot patrol throughout the lot looking for open containers of alcohol, drug paraphernalia (bongs, pipes, papers, etc.). Be aware of alcohol and marijuana odors and their sources. Remember, looking into a vehicle from a place you have a right to occupy (the parking lot) is not a search, with or without a flashlight.

Commonly, officers will run across juveniles on bicycles or skateboards loitering at the park. You should pay particular attention to these groups because juveniles get bored and look for something to do—like burglarize the recreational center or the local school. Use these gatherings to learn names and faces and to gather information on the delinquents in the group.

Examine their bicycles and skateboards for altered or removed serial numbers. These toys have become quite expensive and are frequent targets of juvenile thieves. Use bicycle violations (no license, no lights) to check for serial numbers. Carry sandpaper to remove paint used to cover altered or obliterated serial numbers. Covering, removing, or altering a serial number is a crime. You do not need to prove the bike is stolen to make an arrest in such a case.

PROBABLE CAUSE ARRESTS

After a crime report is taken, a detective supervisor reviews it to determine its solvability. If, according to established guidelines, it has some chance of being solved, it will then be assigned to a detective. The detective has a standard checklist of required duties, such as calling the victim to ensure the details are correct and finding out if he or she has additional information. He will run computer checks on partial and full license plates, nicknames, or anything else unique enough to be checked through the computer.

Depending on the level of work, his experience, and his work ethic, a detective may limit the amount of follow-up. The detective may be successful in identifying the suspect but not have the time to interview him. The detective will then work up an arrest warrant for the suspect if there is probable cause for the warrant. If no probable cause exists but a reasonable suspicion does, a request for contact by patrol officers may be sent out formally (teletype, radio broadcast, etc.). All of this takes time. In the meantime, the suspect has fled, destroyed evidence, or formulated an alibi.

A proactive officer need not wait for an arrest warrant or a request for an interview to be made. If the suspect is identified or can be readily identified and probable cause exists for the arrest, then hit the streets looking for him. Run his name on the computer and find out where he hangs out. Check for other arrest warrants and arrest him out of his house. Add the original charge when booking him into county jail.

The key to these arrests is building a relationship with detectives. Often a suspect is readily identifiable, particularly in a violent crime. The detective just doesn't have the time or manpower to go after him. The detective may take several weeks to get the arrest warrant drafted, approved, and entered into the computer. The next time a detective hears about the case is when a patrol officer picks him up six months later on a routine stop.

Talk to the detectives before going on or after coming off a shift. Enlist the support of your squad in tracking the guy down. If you have problems obtaining information, go to the reports. They are often stacked in some in-basket somewhere. Review them before the start of your shift. You may recognize a nickname, physical description, or M.O. If there

are partial or full license plates, work them through the computer. This type of follow-up can be critical, especially on the weekends when the detectives won't see the reports for several days.

Remember, never assume someone else is working the case. Even the easy ones slide through the cracks.

CAL-ID

In the state of California, a number of police departments have the capability of running suspect fingerprints through a computerized fingerprint file. Currently, the file contains fingerprints obtained from the arrest records of California criminals. California police are using the system to identify suspects who have left prints at various crime scenes (including past crimes) and to identify suspects who are lying about their names.

Such a system offers a street cop the opportunity to initiate innovative ways to attack crime problems. For example, one program initiated involved the use of the system to identify car burglars. Car break-ins are generally considered low-level crimes that receive little or no investigation. However, an energetic group of patrol officers decided to take on the task of fingerprinting all victim vehicles, something not usually done. The prints were then run through the CAL-ID system. The result was an enormous increase in the identification and apprehension of car prowl suspects.

Non-California police officers may wish to use the CAL-ID system to run suspect fingerprints from cases they believe were committed by criminals previously arrested in California. Contact the California Department of Justice in Sacramento for assistance.

One last point on selective enforcement tactics is the futility of random patrol. Undirected patrol is useless.

Have a plan in mind when you leave the station. Establish a route to drive to various targeted areas, including parks, dope houses, and street corners. If one area is "dead," move to the next. Wandering around the beat will not accomplish your goal of arresting crooks. Focusing on their habitats allows you to avoid the majority of law-abiding citizens and concentrate on the ones committing crimes.

SUMMARY

1. Graveyard shift is the perfect time to serve arrest warrants on known street criminals.

2. Use under-the -influence laws to arrest drug dealers.

3. Coordinate drug suppression with officers on your squad.

4. Search likely hiding places at street narcotics sales areas.

5. Stake out narcotics sales areas using binoculars to identify dealers and the location of their stash.

6. Watch their hands.

7. Identify drug-dealing residences and use arrest warrants, minor code violations, and search-and-seizure waivers for enforcement.

8. Take the time to learn minor municipal codes to be used against problem residences.

9. Establish a routine of checking various target areas on your beat between radio calls.

10. Monitor motel parking lots.

11. Don't hesitate to knock and talk.

12. Don't handle needles unnecessarily or carelessly.

13. Walk parking lots of parks using plain-sight observation for legal cause to contact.

14. Check with detectives and fresh cases for active leads on wanted suspects.

ub•ter•fuge *sub'-ter-fyooj'*\\ *n. A deceptive stratagem or device.*

A routine citizen contact: a woman complains that her neighbor is growing marijuana, but she doesn't want to get involved. She can see the plants from her backyard, and she knows what marijuana looks like. So you know the plants are back there, but the question is, how do you get them "legally"?

You figure you have several courses of action: search warrant, plain view, and consent. A search warrant is going to require probable cause (i.e., the citizen's testimony and/or use of her yard to view the plants). This will violate her request for anonymity. Backyard cultivation of marijuana isn't exactly the crime of the century, so you save your "if you don't come forward, how are we going to stop this crime" speech. You give the second option a try. Standing on the sidewalk out front, you jump and crane your neck. You look for public high ground in a vain attempt to obtain a "plain view" sighting of the plants. No go. Well, how about consent? Maybe. But you'll have only one shot at that, so you save that one for last.

That leaves subterfuge. What? This is the slick part of police work that makes it fun.

Abiding by search-and-seizure law is like traversing a minefield with a well-laid-out map in search of contraband. With plenty of time, daylight, and common sense, you can get through (contraband is admissible). But what happens when the minefield you have a map for has all the routes—search warrant, plain view, consent—blocked?

You then begin to rethink the execution of the mission. Your goal is the legal seizure of the plants. Your orientation is to go in legally and grab the plants. But that isn't your only option. You can have the plants brought to you. But who will make the delivery? The neighbor's out. You're out. Well, how about a third party, like the homegrown farmer?

But what in the world is going to motivate this guy to turn over his crop to the police? Fear. Fear of the police. Say that again.

Now I didn't say he would do it willingly; he's just going to be the delivery boy. So the scam develops in your corrupt brain . . . anonymous phone call to the farmer's residence by a seductive female voice: "The cops know about the plants, and they're en route." A couple of well-placed police vehicles are parked near the residence. Five minutes later, here comes a '65 bug out of the suspect's garage.

He spots the marked units, and his face turns pale. Your legal analysis of the above facts gives you "reasonable suspicion" for the traffic stop. At the driver's door you smell the very distinct odor of fresh marijuana coming from the interior of the vehicle. The "movable vehicle" exception to the search warrant requirement allows you to search the vehicle. Bingo—a dozen 5-foot-tall plants.

The arrest isn't going to make the five o'clock news, and your sergeant isn't overly impressed, but damn— you're mightily pleased with yourself.

The use of subterfuge is dependent on each officer's life experience and training. This experience is the basis for the tacks an officer can take. In this vein, an officer is only limited by his imagination. The purpose of this chapter is to highlight true stories of successful uses of subterfuge, illustrating possible methods an officer may use. The stories are self-explanatory.

CHESTER THE MOLESTER

A swing-shift officer going off duty stops by graveyard lineup to brief the lethargic crime fighters on an earlier attempted rape case. It was a late afternoon attack on a 9-year-old girl walking home from school in a suburban middle-class neighborhood. An older man emerges from a parked vehicle, grabs the girl as she is walking by, and attempts to drag her into some bushes. The girl puts up a struggle and a passerby intervenes. The suspect flees on foot, and the police are called. The suspect is at large, unidentified, and the vehicle is still at the scene.

The first question that enters your mind is why the car is still there; it should have been impounded. But then your razor-sharp intellect culls an opportunity from this error in professional judgment. A flash from the past invades your consciousness . . . you're 16, resourceful, and self-employed. Your business—used golf ball recovery at the local aquatic holding ponds. Hours are flexible: summer hours are 1 A.M. to 2 A.M.; winter hours are 4 P.M. to 5 P.M. because it's too cold to be in the water at night. The winter schedule is the most challenging because of the constant aerial restocking of supplies in the water-based warehouse. No problem—reflexes are fine-tuned from constant foot races with the rather competitive security forces.

Lifetime win-loss record is decidedly in your favor. Now, in retrospect, you know the frustration that built up with the competitors' lack of wins. This frustration level eventually led to action. If they couldn't win by direct and fair competition, they would resort to sabotage of your excellent '67 Dodge Coronet. The results of their efforts? A missing coil wire. No wire, no go.

Well, no reason this lesson from the past cannot be used now.

Lineup breaks and first stop is Chester the Molester's

Coil wire in place.

Disconnected coil wire: a fast, effective method of disabling a suspect's vehicle.

vehicle. Out comes the coil wire, and now for some persistence. Radio calls are going to prevent uninterrupted surveillance, but that's not going to stop you from driving by every chance you get.

Tenth trip, 0300, and . . . what do we have here? Looks like a little group mechanics on the "dead" vehicle. Quickly sizing up the membership, you spot Chester

A surreptitious method of disabling a suspect's vehicle is the removal of the rotor and then the replacement of distributor cap.

attempting to crawl into the vehicle's engine compartment. Chester is hooked up, and *damn,* you feel good. You remember why you became a cop.

THAT'S MY CAR

Another graveyard shift and you have the evening planned out. First stop will be 36th Street and Ocean View Boulevard. A junkie convention is going on, and you wave to your favorites rather congenially. Your attention is drawn to a parked car containing three subjects on a side street. Three junkies in a car is a crime wave, so you approach cautiously.

You greet them with your eloquent "What's up" line, and the mandatory "Nothin'" is the response (which, of course, means everything). You check their hands for fragmentation grenades, then move your suspicious scan to the floorboard of the car. On the rear floorboard is a car stereo. Now the game begins.

None of the occupants knows anything about the stereo. Translation: it's stolen. We know it; now try to prove it. Earlier in the evening you had monitored a dispatch to an adjacent beat to take several car burglary reports. This crime scene is close enough to fit this picture. You radio contact the officer taking the report and describe the stereo. He confirms that it is one of the recently stolen stereos. So far so good.

The problem is how to place one of the occupants in "possession" of the stereo. Your only shot is with the owner/driver of the car. According to the occupants, he had disappeared into the nastiest of bars your town has to offer. You enter the bar as if it were the dentist's office and announce the need for the owner's presence back at the car. The crowd responds with the "nice try" look.

Without the driver/owner there will be no arrest. You start to ponder methods by which to pull the driver from his den of security. You know this won't be easy because he's as cautious as a 12-point buck on the second day of deer season. You finally come upon the only lure you have: his car. Take the car and he just might pop his head up.

The tow truck shows up in 15 minutes. It takes the owner 15 seconds to

get from the bar to the car. He wants to
know what is going on, and, of
course, he didn't hear you calling out for the owner. You
point out the car stereo, and he responds with a goofy
"What, me worry?" look. You place him under arrest for
possession of stolen property and make arrangements for
his overnight stay.

The evidence of "possession" isn't exactly over-
whelming, but that's not the point of the story. Scientists
use insect pheromones to attract targeted pests to their
death. This sexual attractant is obviously a powerful
motivator in the bug world. Apply this train of thought to
identify a criminal's motivation or attractant. It may be
an old girlfriend, the lure of easy money, or parenthood.

SUMMARY

1. Use of subterfuge in criminal investigations is both
ethical and proper.

2. There are more ways to handle enforcement problems than the traditional methods. Use your training,
experience, and imagination to develop them.

3. Another officer's incomplete or inept investigation
should not dissuade you from investigating yourself.

4. Drawing a suspect out of hiding requires you to
identify what he values so highly that it is worth the risk
of capture.

CHAPTER 13

LEGAL RECOURSE FOR THE STREET COP

San Diego Police Officer Bill Farrar has a very strong sense of right and wrong. He doesn't believe citizens should be fearful of living out their day-to-day existence and thus takes a strong enforcement stance toward criminals. He also doesn't believe police officers should be used as a community's punching bags. This philosophy provided the impetus for his filing a lawsuit in small-claims court against a drunk who had injured him during an attempt at arresting him.

The radio call that led to Farrar's injury began as a disturbance call. It was a family fight in which the defendant had battered his wife. Prior to Officer Farrar's arrival, the defendant, John Smith (not his true name), had left the scene. The injured wife said her husband was a creature of habit and had more than likely driven to his local watering hole. Officer Farrar drove the short distance to the bar and contacted a subject matching the husband's description. He was sitting at the bar, consuming more alcohol.

The subject identified himself as Smith, and Farrar asked him to step outside. Smith reluctantly did so. Smith was intoxicated so Officer Farrar arrested him for being drunk in public. He placed one handcuff on Smith's wrist. Smith tried to pull away. A struggle ensued when Officer Farrar attempted to place the second handcuff on Smith's other wrist.

Officer Farrar's thumb got caught under the one secured handcuff and was twisted and injured during the struggle. Officer Farrar eventually overcame Smith's resistance and subdued him.

A small crowd of people had gathered to watch the struggle. A few of the bystanders were acquaintances of Smith and were hostile. They viewed Officer Farrar's behavior as inappropriate. Officer Farrar understood that they had a distorted perception of the situation and took the time to explain the original call and the later events. The explanation seemed to calm matters, and a friendly citizen approached Officer Farrar.

The citizen stated he knew Smith and knew that he became hostile when drunk. Thinking ahead, Officer Farrar obtained the citizen's name in case a complaint was filed against him.

Officer Farrar's thumb was sprained, and he missed three days of work. The more he thought about the incident, the more he thought that Smith should pay for his missed work and pain. Small-claims court came to mind as a way to obtain satisfaction. He checked to see if Smith had any assets and learned Smith owned the house Officer Farrar had been called to. Officer Farrar then filed a battery claim against Smith in San Diego Municipal Court's small-claims division.

Officer Farrar alleged his injuries consisted of three days of lost wages, as well as pain and suffering. He filed for the maximum amount for that time period, $1,500. Officer Farrar and the friendly citizen testified on his behalf. Mr. Smith's testimony did not contradict theirs.

Officer Farrar was awarded the $1,500.

He then contacted Mr. Smith's homeowners insurance carrier. He told them the circumstances under which the award was granted. They asked that he send them a copy of the court documents. He did so, and within a week he had a check for $1,500.

When he was interviewed after receiving the judgment, Officer Farrar stated: "I never realized how simple and straightforward the process could be. After this experience, I am no longer going to allow someone to attack or injury me without reprisal. There is no reason the thousands of officers injured each year could not do the same thing."

Police work is like no other job in that few careers call for the employee to place himself in a position to be injured intentionally by others on a continual basis. A patrol officer is especially vulnerable because of the high number of suspects he contacts in often violent and hostile situations. An officer should be aware that he does have civil legal recourse in certain circumstances. There are, however, several special limitations placed on those actions, in particular, the Fireman's Rule and defamation actions.

THE FIREMAN'S RULE

The Fireman's Rule bars a fire fighter or police officer from recovering compensation for injuries sustained because of conduct resulting from his being summoned to the fire, accident, or disturbance. The rule, however, is not unlimited. It does not preclude recovery for acts of misconduct independent of those which necessitated his being summoned.

The Rule's History

The reasons for the rule are threefold: the principle of assumption of risk, the foreseeable risks of employment, and a cost-spreading rationale. The first prevents recovery of damages in tort (a civil wrong) where an individual voluntarily confronts a hazardous situation. The second is based on the rationale that one accepts the inherent hazards of a job when he accepts employment. And finally, recovery is barred in tort because there are other statutory and compensatory schemes available to the fire fighter or police officer.

Limitations on the Rule

Many states, however, have enacted statutes limiting the use of the Fireman's Rule in barring police officer suits. In California, for example, Civil Code section 1714.9 was enacted limiting the applicability of the Fireman's Rule.

Under 1714.9, a police officer may sue in any one of the following situations: if the person knows of or should have known of your presence and does something negligently that results in your being injured; when a person knows of or should have known of your presence and violates a code or statute designed to protect police officers (e.g., battery on a police officer and resisting arrest), and your being injured rests on that conduct; and finally, where the defendant's conduct constitutes arson.

An officer injured on duty can take civil action against one who injures him intentionally. He may also have a cause of action against someone whose negligent conduct causes injury to him after his presence is known, such as an officer injured in a high-speed chase.

DEFAMATION

An officer may also have a legal remedy for someone filing a false complaint against him with his employer. Such a cause of action would fall under the law for defamation suits. In general, however, these suits are often difficult to substantiate due to the strict rules which apply to public officials who are defamed. Police officers are considered public officials, and these same rules apply to them.

The California Rule

Often states have specific statutes which control police officer defamation suits for false complaints. Again, California has such a statute, Civil Code section 47.5.

This rule states that a peace officer may bring an action for defamation against an individual who has filed a complaint with that officer's employing agency alleging misconduct, criminal conduct, or incompetence, if 1) that complaint is false and was made with spite, hatred, or ill will; 2) he has knowledge that the complainant had no reasonable grounds to believe the statement was true; and 3) the complainant exhibited a reckless disregard for ascertaining the truth.

In general, an individual who files a criminal complaint or makes a statement in an official proceeding is protected from a defamation action. Our legislators feel the threat of a defamation suit would dissuade too many honest citizens from coming forward in criminal matters, so such statements are considered privileged. Section 47.5 provides an exception to this rule, but there is a heavy burden of proof on the police officer.

Burden of Proof on the Officer

The officer must prove the following: the complaint was false, the citizen knew it was false, and the complaint was made with ill will. Often times the citizen complaints boil down to the citizen's word against the officer's. When this is the case, the officer doesn't have a chance under 47.5.

Tips for Success

Officers who are thorough in identifying witnesses, obtaining incriminating statements from the citizen or witnesses, and ensuring that other officers are present during threats of reprisal are more likely to have a winnable case. The best suggestion I can offer, however, is the use of a tape recorder.

Get a belt clip for a microrecorder or throw a standard-size one in your bag. Suspects tend to get their mouthiest when they're behind the cage and en route to the drunk tank/jail, so flipping the switch on the machine sitting next to you shouldn't be a problem. Besides, it makes great play at lineup the next day.

SMALL-CLAIMS COURT

Besides the statutory limitations placed on police officer lawsuits, there are also practical barricades to consider. Due to the intricacies of the civil system, an injured police officer would require the services of an attorney in order to navigate the legal labyrinth. Attorneys work for an hourly rate of between $75 to $300 an hour, or they may elect to accept a case on a contingency basis. A contingency fee is a percentage of the final judgment less costs, usually between 33 and 40 percent of the award.

Police officers generally cannot afford to pay an hourly rate for any substantial amount of time. They are then left with the contingency fee option. However, an attorney accepting a case on such a basis first considers the value of the case and the likelihood of collecting any judgment. People who batter police officers are not usually high-wage earners, so finding an attorney to accept such a case is rare.

Even if an officer finds an attorney willing to take his case, the attorney cannot guarantee results. Rules of professional conduct prevent attorneys from making such guarantees. These rules are important in controlling the sales pitches attorneys make to prospective clients.

The problem then is, how you can sue the middle-class drunk who took a chunk of skin off your forearm? I suggest small-claims court, where attorneys are not allowed.

Award Limitations

Current small-claims court judgment limits are $2,500 and $5,000. You may file two claims a year for up to $5,000 and an unlimited number for up to $2,500. These limits open the door for a number of suits that arise out of day-to-day police work, such as the spitting drunk, the foot to the groin, or the false citizen complaint.

Case Analysis

Before you take any affirmative

steps in pursuing the case, I suggest
you analyze the case much the same
way an attorney would. First, what is the legal liability
theory you would be filing on (e.g., battery, defamation,
intentional infliction of emotional harm)? Second, what
evidence do you have to establish the elements of the
offense (e.g., witness availability, medical reports, tape
recordings, photos, etc.)? Third, what is the extent of
injury (none, little, or just anger)? Visible physical injuries
are not always necessary, even in a battery case, but be
prepared to articulate the pain or emotional distress you
suffered. And finally, but most importantly, what is the
feasibility of recovering any judgment?

Judgment Recovery

When evaluating the feasibility of collecting, keep in
mind what the source of funds for payment would be:
garnisheed wages, lien on residence, or insurance policies. Homeowners insurance policies will cover some
tort damages.

Often the key to recovery is establishing where the
defendant is employed and whether he owns any real
property, such as a house or land. From the arrest, you
probably will already know if and where he is employed.
To locate any real property, a trip to the county recorder's
office is in order. Such information is public record and
is filed by name as well as by parcel number.

Judgment Creditor Examination

There is also a legal proceeding called a "judgment
creditor examination," which may help locate the
defendant's assets. After the trial, the defendant is
required to answer questions regarding his assets. If he
refuses to answer, the judge may find him in contempt
of court.

If these methods are inadequate or unsuccessful, a call
to a private detective may be in order. They routinely conduct asset checks on individuals, usually through computer systems that access reporting agencies such as TRW.

Case Preparation
An officer can expect to spend a minimum of six to eight hours preparing his case for court. The officer must be willing to learn the applicable law well enough to explain it to the judge and incorporate it into his presentation. He must be willing to contact and interview possible witnesses. These witnesses must then be served

---

COURT USE ONLY: Hrg date:_____   Pymt:CS/CK/MO $ _____   Service:_____

EL CAJON MUNICIPAL COURT, SMALL CLAIMS DIVISION, EL CAJON JUDICIAL DISTRICT
COUNTY OF SAN DIEGO, STATE OF CALIFORNIA

PLAINTIFF'S STATEMENT WORKSHEET (#310)

INSTRUCTIONS: Complete both sides of this form and give it to the clerk for processing. NOTE: If there are additional plaintiffs/defendants or the parties are doing business under another name (DBA) or are known under another name (AKA) you must complete the green Supplemental Statement worksheet (in addition to this form) and give both forms to the clerk.

INFORMATION ABOUT YOU (PLAINTIFF)
(4) Print Plaintiff's First Name, Middle Initial, Last Name, or Name of Business. Is this a business? Circle YES/NO.

|_|_|_|_|_|_|_|_|_|_|_|_|_|_|_|_|_|_|_|_|_|_|_|_|_|_|_|_|_|_|_|_|

(8) Print Name Description, e.g., a California Corporation, a Sole Proprietorship if applicable.

|_|_|_|_|_|_|_|_|_|_|_|_|_|_|_|_|_|_|_|_|_|_|_|_|_|_|_|_|_|_|_|_|

(9) Plaintiff Address: |_|_|_|_|_|_|_|_|_|_|_|_|_|_|_|_|_|_|_|_|_|_|

(10) City: |_|_|_|_|_|_|_|_|_|_|_|_|_|_|_|_|_|_|_|_|_|_|
State: |_|_|_| Zip: |_|_|_|_|_|

NOTE: If there are additional plaintiffs, AKAs or DBAs you must complete green Supplemental Statement form.

INFORMATION ABOUT THE PARTY YOU ARE SUING (DEFENDANT)
(5) Whom is your claim against? Is this a business?   Circle YES/NO

|_|_|_|_|_|_|_|_|_|_|_|_|_|_|_|_|_|_|_|_|_|_|_|_|_|_|_|_|_|_|_|_|

(19) Print Name Description, e.g., a California Corporation, a Sole Proprietorship if applicable.

|_|_|_|_|_|_|_|_|_|_|_|_|_|_|_|_|_|_|_|_|_|_|_|_|_|_|_|_|_|_|_|_|

(20) Defendant Address: |_|_|_|_|_|_|_|_|_|_|_|_|_|_|_|_|_|_|_|_|_|_|

(21) City: |_|_|_|_|_|_|_|_|_|_|_|_|_|_|_|_|_|_|_|_|_|
State: |_|_|_| Zip: |_|_|_|_|_|

Note: If there are additional defendants, AKAs or DBAs you must complete green Supplemental Statement form.

INFORMATION ABOUT YOUR CLAIM
(24) Does the defendant live in San Diego County? Circle YES/NO.

(25) This is the proper court for the hearing because: (check appropriate box)
    [ ] A. a defendant lives in this judicial district or a defendant corporation or unincorporated association has its principal place of business in the judicial district.

    [ ] B. a person was injured or personal property was damaged in this judicial district.

    [ ] C. a defendant signed or entered into a contract in this judicial district, a defendant lived in this judicial district when the contract was entered into, a contract or obligation was to be performed in this judicial district, or, if the defendant was a corporation, the contract was breached in this judicial district.

    [ ] D. the claim is on a retail installment account or contract subject to Civil Code Section 1812.10. Specify facts:
    _____

    [ ] E. the claim is on a vehicle finance sale subject to Civil Code Section 2984.4. Specify facts:
    _____

SC-36
(3-92) [ ] F. other. Specify facts:_____

A simple fill-in-the-blank small-claims court complaint form allows nonlawyer police officers easy access to the civil court system.

with subpoenas. After a review of the facts and the law, the officer must formulate a logical presentation. The most effective and comprehensible format is a time-sequence one. This boils down to simply telling the story as it occurred.

First Step: Demand Letter

After establishing you have a viable case, the first step is to send a demand letter to the defendant. State the reason for the demand and the amount owed. Send

---

(24) Amount of your claim (*do not include court costs*): $ |_|,|_|_| |_| |_|.|_| |_|

(27) Date incurred: |__|__| |__|__| |__|__|
  MO   DA   YR

(28) Print name of person who will sign this form _____

(31) Nature of Action:

|_|_|_|_|_|_|_|_|_|_|_|_|_|_|_|_|_|_|_|_|_|_|_|_|_|_|_|_|_|_|_|_|_|_|_|_|_|_|_|_|_|_|_|_|

NOTE: If this claim involves a vehicle accident or an unlawful detainer you must complete green Supplement Statement Form.

INFORMATION ABOUT YOUR HEARING DATE (#350)

A. Do you wish this matter to be heard in our Ramona Branch at 1428 Montecito Road in Ramona, CA?

Circle YES/NO
If YES, your trial will be set on a Friday at 9:00 a.m.

B. Does the defendant live outside of the County of San Diego? Circle YES/NO
If YES, your trial date will be set in approximately 40 days.
If NO, your trial date will be set in approximately 30 days.

C. Trials are scheduled as follows. Please write your 1st and 2nd choice of the court day and time below:

TUESDAY	WEDNESDAY	THURSDAY	FRIDAY
8:00 a.m.	8:00 a.m.	8:00 a.m.	8:00 a.m.
10:00 a.m.	10:00 a.m.	10:00 a.m.	10:00 a.m.
1.00 p.m.	1:00 p.m.	1:00 p.m.	1:00 p.m.
3:00 p.m.	3:00 p.m.	3:00 p.m.	3:00 p.m.
	5:00 p.m.		

1st choice_____ 2nd choice _____

==

NOTICE TO PLAINTIFF

The cost to file a small claim is $8.00 each or $16.00 if more than one other small claims action has been filed anywhere in California during this calendar year in which the amount demanded is more than $2,500.00. If you cannot afford the filing fee for filing a small claim case or the cost of serving the claim on the other party, you should tell the clerk. You will be given a form that you can fill out and sign to request that the Court permit you to file your case without paying the fees. You may talk to any attorney, however, you cannot be represented by an attorney at the time of trial in the small claims division.

A small claims advisor is available to give assistance without charge. The service is available to both plaintiffs and defendants. Neither the county nor the advisors may be held liable for any losses as a result of advice give to either party. *If you want advisor assistance you may call 236-2700 for information.*

YOU HAVE NO RIGHT TO APPEAL FROM A JUDGMENT ON YOUR CLAIM.

by registered mail, return receipt requested. If he fails to respond, then the next step is to file a complaint with the court. Most county courthouses have small-claims divisions.

Second Step: File Complaint

The initial form is called a complaint and is in a simple check-the-box-type format. In California, the fee to file the complaint is $8. At this time, you select the method by which the defendant is to be served notice of the suit, either by registered mail ($5), by the county marshal ($21), or by any uninvolved adult. Registered mail is the least successful method of service. Personal service by the marshal or others is your best bet.

Once the defendant is served with the complaint, he is required to appear in court on the date set. If he fails to appear, default judgment is entered. You win the amount you have stated in the complaint. If he appears, then it is simply a matter of both of you presenting your cases.

Case Presentation

This part is right out of "The People's Court." In fact, as corny as this sounds, I suggest you watch a few episodes to get an idea of the type of evidence preferred and how it should be presented.

A point you should keep in mind while presenting your case is the experience of the judges hearing small-claims matters. Often they are "judge pro tems," which means they are attorneys who are appointed to hear such cases on a temporary basis but are not judges. If yours is a matter that involves some of the unique aspects of police work, be prepared to educate the judge in those areas.

In particular are California Civil Code section 47.5 (defamation actions by police officers) and 1714.9 (exemptions from the Fireman's Rule). These are unusual sections, and it's almost guaranteed that the judge will not have dealt with them previously or will have a mistaken belief as to their legal effects. Obtain a copy of the sections from a law library for yourself and the judge.

If you win the case and judgment is entered for you, the most difficult aspect of the suit may be collecting the judgment. You first must wait 30 days before you may begin collection efforts. If the defendant still refuses to pay, you may obtain what is called a "writ of execution" to garnishee his wages. This document is served on his employer, who is then required to make payments from the defendant's wages to you.

Abstract of Judgment

A second method of collection is obtaining an "abstract of judgment," which is again obtained from the court and then filed with the county recorder's office. This places a lien on any real property the defendant may own. Before he is able to sell this property or refinance it, he must have the lien removed by satisfying his debt to you.

Records

Throughout your case, keep detailed records of your communications with the defendant. Use registered mail to ensure that he is receiving any legal notices you have sent out. During each request before the court, you will have to substantiate that the defendant has had notice and there is a need for court action to enforce the judgment.

No Guarantees

Success in small-claims court is never guaranteed. The personal bias of the judge, as well as his interpretation of the law, may greatly affect the outcome. Recovery of the full amount sued for is also not certain for the same reasons. The small fees charged, however, make small claims court an attractive legal avenue.

* * * * *

One final point on small-claims court. The criminal system has obviously failed in dissuading citizens from bashing police officers. Police administrators, district attorneys, and police unions are either uninterested or incapable of protecting police officers from such abuses. If such attacks are to prevented or punished, it is up to the individual officer to look after his own interest. Remember, grab them in the wallet, and their hearts and minds will follow.

SUMMARY

1. Once a person is aware of a police officer's presence and he intentionally or negligently injures the officer, he may then be civilly liable to the officer.

2. Anticipate civil litigation in all incidents, whether you are the plaintiff or the defendant.

3. Identify all witnesses to the incident.

4. Use a tape recorder to protect yourself from unsubstantiated complaints.

5. Identify the source of funds to be used to pay any judgment you may receive before you initiate legal action.

6. Be prepared to educate a judge on the law.

CHAPTER 14

SPECIAL EQUIPMENT

here are a number of specialty items available to the "street cop" that you will not normally find in a patrol officer's gear bag. First, let's talk high tech.

VIDEO CAMERAS/TAPE RECORDERS

The nature of street work focuses on arrests often based soley on the police officer's observations and testimony. Faced with a defendant willing to take the stand, the case boils down to the officer's word against the defendant's. The defense attorney's role in the scenario consists of his efforts to destroy the credibility of the officer. He does this by implying the officer could not have seen, heard, or smelled what he has testified to. Or he may introduce witnesses (prior arrestees of the officer) who testify to his improper conduct in their cases.

To combat the "trial of the officer," an officer needs to employ objective recording devices that provide substantive proof of the defendant's conduct. Video recorders and tape recorders are such devices.

Many police agencies employ the use of dash-mounted and hand-held video recorders for use in drunk driving arrests. These have proven to be very effective in resolving these types of cases. A street cop may wish to employ the same method. Home video recorders often go unused for lengthy periods of time between weddings and birthday parties.

Take the time to adapt a mount to your police car dashboard and tape record routine traffic stops. Once a scene is secure, walk the camera around a residence to be searched to give your perspective on the plain-sight observation that led to the warrant. The idea of patrol officers using video cameras is fairly new, but after several recent well-publicized videotapings, cameras should become almost as prominent as ticket books in patrol cars.

Tape recorders have been well-established patrol

A self-installed video camera provides not only objective recording of events but also great memories.

officer tools for a number of years.
The most popular styles are the
hand-held standard cassette type and
the microrecorders for your gun belt.

Both serve the function of tape recording reports,
secretly recording suspects' conversations while sitting
in the back seat of your car, and recording the demands
and threats of a volatile detainee. One of these should be
standard equipment in every patrol officer's bag.

PAGERS

Drug dealers have recognized the necessity of pagers
and so should the patrol officer. Officers receive quite a
bit of information from citizens and informants during a
shift. However, this information often requires a follow-
up contact to the citizen. For example, you're assisting
detectives in tracking down a purse-snatching suspect
who has been identified. You show his photo to a 7-11
clerk who recognizes him as someone who hangs out
there on Friday nights. You don't have the time or
manpower to stake the place out, so you give the clerk
your pager number. You tell him to punch in a
designated code, 711, followed by 911. Within two
hours you get the page, and the suspect is soon in
custody. The pager saves both the citizen and the officer
the needless delay and confusion of going through
dispatch. The pager gives citizens immediate access to
an officer already versed in the details of the crime, and
it avoids the distastefulness of giving out your home
phone number.

NARCOTIC TEST KITS

These test kits (plastic envelope, glass-vial type)
initially serve as reinforcers for the novice officer
involved in drug arrests. A powder may be recovered
from a suspect who claims it is "cut," as opposed to the
drug itself. The officer can run a test to reassure himself
it is the drug he suspects it to be. With time, however,
the officer learns one of the most accurate methods of

identifying a powder as a controlled substance is the packaging of the powder. Dopers don't usually package cut in balloons, viles, or aluminum unless they're selling "bunk" (fake) dope. Once an officer's confidence builds, he will rely less on the test kits.

There are several problems with test kits. The kits are expensive and rapidly used up. Most important, though, is the destruction of the controlled substance during the testing. A balloon of heroin contains a fraction of a gram of powder or tar. After field testing, there may not be enough for the police lab to test and later have admitted into court. Keep these limitations in mind when using field narcotic test kits.

FIELD INTERVIEW FILES

Field interview slips often come with a copy designated for use by the patrol officer. Judicious retention of copies of field interview slips on habitual criminals in your area will reinforce knowledge of their identities, residences, vehicles, and habits. Occasional review may initiate warrant checks or allow for immediate identification verification on the street.

Be careful in retaining photographs with the files. Such photo files are not necessarily illegal as long as access is limited to sworn personnel and they are kept secure. However, many police departments have regulations delineating who or what division may maintain such a file.

CAMERAS

Polaroids offer the fastest verification of the usefulness of the picture taken. A picture of track marks or a weapon can be sent immediately to the district attorney's office along with the arrest report. However, there are quite a few advantages to 35mm film. For one, it's a lot cheaper. Second, the quality of the photograph

Hand mirrors, screw-
drivers, sandpaper, leg
restraints, and small
flashlights should all be a
part of a street cop's
gear bag.

is usually quite a bit better. Whichever type you use,
remember, many a prosecutor has said, "There never
can be too many photographs."

MISCELLANEOUS TOOLS

A small square of sandpaper should be kept to
remove painted over, removed, or disguised serial
numbers on bicycles and vehicles. A straight-edge
screwdriver can be used to open vehicle trunks that
have had the lock removed. The trunk latch is usually
still operational and has a slot that the screwdriver can
be fitted into and turned to open the trunk. A pen light
can be used to examine pupil size and response. A tie-
down for the trunk of your car is handy for impounding
a recovered stolen bicycle.

SUMMARY

1. Use your home video camera on patrol. It's both fun and provides strong evidence in a criminal prosecution.

2. A tape recorder can be a cop's best friend. Keep one in your gear bag.

3. Pagers provide a quick and safe method of communication between an officer and citizens or informants.

4. Narcotic tests kits are invaluable in reinforcing the training of a novice officer.

5. A field interview file is useful in learning the names, faces, and addresses of local street criminals.

6. Carry a camera, regardless of the model, to preserve evidence that lends itself to photographing.

CONCLUSION

he philosophy behind this book is that patrol officers should be relentless in their pursuit of criminals. Every time an officer leaves the station, makes a traffic stop, or conducts a field interview, he should be thinking of ways to lock the street thug up. For the more sensitive among you, I'm not talking about arresting Grandma Walton or Beaver Cleaver. I'm talking about the career criminal, from the ex-con to the junkie.

In fact, a patrol officer should minimize the contact he has with Joe Citizen. A patrol officer has limited time in a shift. Use the time you have to focus on the source of the pain and hurt in society, the street criminal.

Street Cop provides information on criminal recognition, criminal identification, and criminal apprehension techniques. With this information, an officer will be able to scan an area containing a number of people and quickly eliminate 90 percent of the group from scrutiny. He should then be able to focus immediately on the one or two subjects who show criminal potential. Once the officer contacts the suspect, he should focus on the suspect's potential and the probable cause necessary to search and arrest him.

This is a hard-core philosophy directed at a hard-core criminal element. I am not apologetic about it, and neither should you be. Keep it in mind when you're holding the hand of the 79-year-old grandmother who just had her hip broken during a violent purse snatch. Criminals belong in jail, where they have no one to hurt but themselves.

The biggest barrier you will have in employing this philosophy is your own timidness about doing things that are unpleasant or that are thought of as rude. This includes peering into parked vehicles, stopping vehicles for minor violations, interrogating uncooperative criminals, and insisting on searching vehicles that have a marijuana roach in the ashtray.

How long will it take to overcome this timidness? As soon as you find your first convict with a loaded 9mm under his seat and a stocking mask in his pocket. The more of these stops you make, the more success you will have and the more confidence you will build. Pretty soon you will start making some awesome arrests of some terrible individuals.

The label "good street cop" is one of the highest compliments an officer can pay a fellow police officer. *Street Cop*, the book, provides the tactics and resources necessary to earn this title. It is now up to you whether you want to make the effort.

onovan Jacobs is a retired San Diego police officer with more than 13 years of experience in law enforcement. He retired due to injuries from a gunshot wound and recently graduated from law school. He is currently an attorney practicing in San Diego.

He spent the majority of his career working selective enforcement units targeting narcotics abusers. His assignments included the Narcotics Street Team, Southeast Enforcement Team, Beach Enforcement Team, and SWAT. He is a court-recognized narcotics expert.

He has two regularly published columns in the San Diego Police Officers' Association newspaper, *The Informant* (circ. 20,000), and has been published in nationwide police publications. *Street Cop* is his first published book.